WRITING FOR COLLEGE

GEORGIA ENGLISH AND WRITING EXAMS

LINDA L. ARTHUR
Georgia Southern University

HUBERT C. PULLEY
Georgia Southern University

KENDALL/HUNT PUBLISHING COMPANY
4050 Westmark Drive   Dubuque, Iowa 52002

Upper left photo, second photo from the top on the right, and center photo © 2002 PhotoDisc, Inc.

Copyright © 2002 by Linda L. Arthur and Hubert C. Pulley

ISBN 0-7872-9471-3

Kendall/Hunt Publishing Company has the exclusive rights to reproduce this work,
to prepare derivative works from this work, to publicly distribute this work,
to publicly perform this work and to publicly display this work.

All rights reserved. No part of this publication may be reproduced,
stored in a retrieval system, or transmitted, in any form or by any
means, electronic, mechanical, photocopying, recording, or otherwise,
without the prior written permission of Kendall/Hunt Publishing Company.

Printed in the United States of America
10 9 8 7 6 5 4 3 2 1

TABLE OF CONTENTS

PREFACE	v
CHAPTER ONE: WHY DIDN'T I PASS THE EXIT EXAM?	1
A Checklist	9
CHAPTER TWO: GRAMMAR	11
Mastery Test One	25
CHAPTER THREE: PUNCTUATION	29
Mastery Test Two	41
CHAPTER FOUR: SENTENCE STRUCTURE	45
Mastery Test Three	61
CHAPTER FIVE: DICTION AND STYLE	63
Mastery Test Four	77
PRACTICE EXIT EXAMS	81
General Directions for Practice Exit Exams	82
PRACTICE EXIT EXAM ONE	83
PRACTICE EXIT EXAM TWO	91
PRACTICE EXIT EXAM THREE	101
PRACTICE EXIT EXAM FOUR	111
PRACTICE EXIT EXAM FIVE	121
PRACTICE EXIT EXAM SIX	131
PRACTICE EXIT EXAM SEVEN	141
PRACTICE EXIT EXAM EIGHT	153
PRACTICE EXIT EXAM NINE	163
PRACTICE EXIT EXAM TEN	173
SCANTRONS FOR PRACTICE EXIT EXAMS	181
CHAPTER SIX: WRITING THE EXIT ESSAY	203
Practice Exit Exam: Outline and Essay	232
CHAPTER SEVEN: TYPES OF ESSAYS	237

GENERAL GUIDELINES FOR WRITING EXIT ESSAYS	**261**
SUGGESTED TOPICS FOR TYPES OF ESSAYS	**262**
ANSWER KEYS FOR CHAPTERS AND PRACTICE EXIT EXAMS	**265**
REFERENCES FOR CHAPTERS	**299**
REFERENCES FOR PRACTICE EXIT EXAMS	**301**

PREFACE

It is with pleasure that we present *Writing for College: Georgia English and Writing Exams* to fellow educators across the state of Georgia. The publication of this text is significant for four reasons: 1) the text is specifically geared toward students trying to master Georgia writing tests for entrance into the university system; 2) it is the first text for this target group that includes chapter material explaining the skills needed to pass standardized English entrance or exit examinations; 3) it presents formats for plenty of writing practice; and 4) it has features not found in other practice writing test materials and which have proved through classroom experience to be of great benefit for the student attempting to master these types of tests.

The style of the book is aimed at maximizing student success. The explanatory sections of the text are informal and easy to read. The ten Practice Exit Exams have been written with assessments such as the College Placement Exam (CPE) and the COMPASS in mind. Most passages are about 250 to 300 words, and the majority of the test passages are drawn from college textbooks and other college-level materials. Test passages include narrative and expository selections–the latter presenting topics from the humanities, social sciences, and health sciences. In addition, a crucial feature of the text is that the students have a chance to practice writing different types of exit essays.

This text was designed to be a helpful tool in classrooms with varied methodologies. We hope that the book serves our colleagues as well as our students in Departments of Learning Support throughout the state of Georgia.

Acknowledgement: We want to express our gratitude to a contributing author, Mildred Pate, for her valuable work on this text.

CHAPTER ONE:
WHY DIDN'T I PASS THE EXIT EXAM?

TAKING EXIT EXAMINATIONS

Taking exit examinations can be nerve-racking. Have you ever thought about why students get tense before exams, especially ones such as the *College Placement Exam* (the CPE) or the *COMPASS*? Have you ever thought, said, or overheard any of the following comments in your learning support classes?

"I did exactly what the teacher told me, and I still failed the test!"
"Nobody told me if I didn't pass one part, it would keep me from getting out of Learning Support!"
"When I saw those other students finish their tests before I did, I knew I was too slow."
"Man, when that teacher wrote '10 minutes' on the board, my mind went blank. I know my whole last paragraph crashed and burned."
"I left the last ten circles blank. I didn't know they would count against me."

Why do students continue to put themselves through this agony? *They know that educational success is one way to elevate social status and achieve security.* At the same time, however, the requirement of taking these tests and passing them sets into motion the idea of the "Do or Die" syndrome.

In order to elevate social status and achieve security, educational success is, indeed, imperative. In Georgia, the Board of Regents has mandated that in order to enter college, students must make a certain score on the SAT and have a certain high school grade point average. Students who don't achieve these scores (i.e., satisfy the formula for the Freshman Index) are required to take placement tests; the students who do not pass the placement tests are consequently placed in Developmental Studies or Learning Support classes. During and/or at the end of their first semester, these same students must take an exit exam in order to be admitted as a regular student. This mandated test-taking process creates a tremendous amount of pressure on the student.

As mentioned, educational success is crucial to one's success as perceived by society. Traditionally, students who attend college are held in high esteem by the general public because these students have elected to continue to study beyond the post secondary level: to expand their knowledge and to become more specialized. Once these students graduate from college, they continue to be looked upon as successful individuals who will make great strides to top levels in their fields. Conversely, someone who does not complete college may be viewed as unsuccessful. Placing such emphasis on one event (i.e., the exit examination) generates tension for the student (and to a much lesser extent even the instructor). Thus, this one-shot principle that leads a student to think, "I have to pass or I won't get into college; I won't be qualified for a good job, and I'll never be able to make a decent living" may infiltrate a student's psyche so that s/he believes one's entire career depends upon success in a single event. This event, the exit exam, does determine a student's admission to or rejection from a college–this part is true, but students tend to believe that failing the exit exam could be the "end" of them and their ability to have a good life. The obsession to enter college may be due to the one-shot principle. Students may feel they have little chance of returning to formal education once they fail the exit exam (even though, in most cases, they are given more than one chance to pass it). Perhaps students feel that more than any other single event, the exit exam determines their career path. Certainly the kind of future employment they are counting on depends upon it, and their status in society is shaped by it. Since most Developmental Studies students feel "stupid" for even having to take remedial classes, the failure to exit the Developmental Studies program could have lasting psychological effects. So, no wonder students are nervous about taking these tests!

Exercise 1. Reflect for a moment. What other important events do you believe are viewed as "one-shot" chances? Write them in the space provided.

_____

_____

DISPELLING NERVOUS TENSION

How can you dispel the nervous tension surrounding major tests, especially exit exams? One of the best ways to calm yourself is to *realize that even if you do not pass the exam, it is not "the end" of your life.* Of course, it would be ideal for you to pass, and by preparing yourself, you will have a better chance of being successful. This text will help you prepare academically, but you also have to do your part.

Another way of dispelling nervousness is to have an acceptable Plan B in mind in case you don't do as well as you had hoped: 1) know how many times you are allowed to take the test (at many institutions you may have up to three semesters to pass the exam); 2) make calls to other colleges to find out what admission requirements are (be sure to tell them you are currently in a Developmental Studies program); 3) make calls to technical schools in the area to scope out whether or not those institutions have majors in fields in which you are interested; and 4) consider working for a semester or two until you can make a firm decision about your future. Knowing that you have other acceptable and appropriate options will calm you down. Now you are ready to truly prepare yourself physically, emotionally, and logistically for the exam.

PREPARING PHYSICALLY, EMOTIONALLY, AND LOGISTICALLY FOR THE EXAM

Why did you fail the last exit exam you took? Can you take an honest look at this question? What were you doing the night before the exam? What you did may have affected your performance on the test.

Exercise 2. Consider the following checklist of possible behaviors. Check the items that apply to your behavior before the day of the exit exam or the morning of the exam.

_____1. Went out drinking

_____2. Indulged in some type of substance abuse

_____3. Got only a few hours of sleep

_____4. Didn't eat

_____5. Drank a lot of coffee

_____6. Forgot to take my prescription medications

_____7. Went to my classes and got tired out

_____8. Talked with my parents and had a fight

_____9. Talked with my boy/girlfriend and had a fight

_____10. Got emotionally upset by someone (for example, roommate, teacher, guy at the convenience store)

_____11. Took an attitude of "I can pass it; I just don't want to"

_____12. Took an attitude of being angry at even having to take the "ridiculous test"

_____13. Didn't feel focused when I arriving at the test site

_____14. Was rushing

_____15. Couldn't find the exam location

_____16. Forgot my I.D., pencils

____17. Couldn't sit in the spot I wanted

____18. Got disturbed by others making noise in the room

____19. Forgot my watch

____20. Other: _____

Your path to being successful on the exit exam will depend a great deal on what you checked in Exercise 2. The following chart will alert you to the area you should focus on for self-improvement, whether it be physical, emotional, or logistical. (We are assuming that all students want to focus on the academic aspect of the test, and we have devoted the remainder of this textbook to that aspect.)

Exercise 3. Circle the numbers below that you checked in Exercise 2.

Physical	Emotional	Logistical
1 2 3 4 5	8 9 10 11 12	14 15 16 17
6 7 Other:	13 Other:	18 19 Other:

Scoring. The "box" in which you circled the most items is the aspect you need to focus on. Below you will find a discussion of each area and suggestions for improving in those areas.

PHYSICAL ASPECTS OF TEST-TAKING

According to Arthur (1996) and others, a certain amount of test anxiety is normal and can even be beneficial in two ways: 1) it will prompt you to prepare for the test; and 2) it will, during the test, prompt you to concentrate and work efficiently. However, if you are so anxious that you can't eat, rest, focus, or prepare before the test, or you are a nervous wreck during the test, you need to overcome this anxiety in order to perform well on the exam. A further way to dispel your anxiety is to prepare yourself physically.

The physical symptoms of anxiety can sometimes be controlled through diet and nutrition and sleep. It is well known that a lack of sleep leads to listlessness, drowsiness, and the inability to concentrate. But did you know that it can also lead to a feeling of doom? Eating unbalanced meals may also act as a catalyst for such symptoms. Try eating nutritionally balanced meals beginning two weeks before the test as well as getting a good night's sleep (preferably eight hours) days in advance. It is obvious that being alert rather than sleepy can make a difference in answering items correctly.

In addition, if you are on any prescription medications as a part of your lifestyle, be sure to take them as prescribed. Alternating days or forgetting to take your medicine can be disastrous. Further, avoid the "trap" of escapism. As a student, you do have responsibilities: don't escape from them through substance abuse. The test will still face you, and you will put yourself at a disadvantage if you have to recuperate from a hangover.

Finally, while taking the test, you may experience panic and its symptoms—trembling, breathlessness, and sweating. To overcome this, know that breath control can ease hyperventilation. (Hyperventilation decreases the carbon dioxide in your blood, creating a chemical imbalance.) If your breathing becomes rapid, focus on breathing in and out slowly. The point here is that you want to keep your physical being at its optimal level. Take care of yourself.

-Arthur, et. al., p. 69

PREPARING EMOTIONALLY FOR THE EXAM

One of the biggest obstacles to feeling confident for the exam is the existence of "mind tapes." Beliefs about yourself, if negative, can be detrimental to your cause. For example, if you are in a social situation trying to impress a person of the opposite sex, and you stumble and fall all over yourself, knocking into another person who spills her drink, what does your mind tell you? Write what comes to mind:

_____

_____

Some answers to this question might include: "I'm so stupid! Everyone is going to think I'm drunk! I can't even keep my balance! I'm so clumsy! I'll never get a boy/girlfriend at this rate! I've never impressed anyone! No one will ever like me! I'll never fit in! I can't face them tomorrow!"

Have you ever wondered why most of our thoughts are negative? These statements could be part of your mind tapes, and if you take a good look at them, you could probably see that all of them are false! For example, are you really stupid? How could you have possibly gotten as far as college if that were the truth about you? And what about the statement, "No one will ever like me." Can you truly say that no one likes you, ever has, or ever will? When you stumbled and spilled your drink, why didn't your mind just say, "Oops!". . . and let it go?

What triggers mind tapes to play? In some cases people who are close to you trigger them, usually unintentionally: girlfriends, boyfriends, parents, siblings, friends, and roommates. Until you have gotten control of or eliminated your "triggers," it may be best to avoid confrontations before you take the exit exam. Call your loved ones immediately *after* the exam, not before. If you need to, spend the night away from your residence hall so your roommate won't have the chance to get on your nerves. Also consider that if you are with your boyfriend the night before the exam and have a fight, what kind of emotional state will you be in to take the test? Merely saying, "I don't care" to yourself isn't going to work. You probably do care, and you will worry about the situation throughout the exam. In one week you may be back together, and you might not have done well on the exit exam (an important event) because of that fight.

Start *NOW* to control your mind tapes and eventually even eliminate them. *They are false tapes* that most everyone has carried in his or her head at one time or another. If you believe you are carrying a tape that echoes "I am stupid; that's why I'm in Developmental Studies/Learning Support," or "I will never pass this test," *get rid of it; it is false information.* Replace it with one that repeats, "I have prepared for this test for a semester, and I'm ready to take it on. I will pass this test."

When you find your mind dwelling on or repeating negative ideas, make yourself negate those ideas. You could even say "Stop!" in your head. Concentrate instead on how hard you have worked to prepare for the test, tell yourself you will do your best job, and remember you have intelligently created a Plan B which is in place, ready to be implemented.

PRACTICALITIES

In order to make sure you are successful in taking and passing exit exams, there are several practical considerations you can put in place for yourself:

1. Visit the building and room a week before the test to ensure that you find the exam room with no problem; if you can't find parking, or if you are running late, at least you will know how to go directly to the room.

2. If noises bother you (coughing, sneezing, pencil-tapping, etc.) buy earplugs. Get the kind that swimmers wear (the softer kind). Practice wearing your earplugs during class practice test sessions.

3. Stop drinking and stop all substance abuse a week before the examination. It takes a few days for your body (and mind) to rid itself of these kinds of substances.

4. Don't eat strange foods the night before the test, and don't drink too much coffee the morning of the exam. You can't afford to be making trips to the

restroom. Men may lose up to 4 minutes, and women may lose up to 7 minutes of test time.

5. Buy candy to take during the test. Because some experts say that your blood sugar level goes down after 25 minutes of concentrating, eating some hard candy at the half-way point is a good idea. Be sure to have your candy already unwrapped and already on your desk so that you don't disturb others during the exam. If candy is not permitted in the room, you might want to take cough drops (they have about the same amount of sugar in them).

6. Don't wear any new clothes or shoes. You don't want anything taking your attention away from the questions in front of you.

7. Take all prescribed medications regularly at least one to two weeks before the test. Don't put your body in any kind of yo-yo state.

8. For a few days before the test, eat protein. Some experts say it is good for your brain power. (Cheese and red meat or chicken contain protein; if you need breakfast, a sausage biscuit or eggs should suffice.)

9. Arrive on time to the test. You will not feel comfortable if you arrive late. If you are flustered, you will have to take time to calm yourself first and may lose valuable time. If you arrive early, you can settle yourself and do some breathing exercises.

10. Wear a watch. You will have practiced timing yourself during class practice tests, and all your practice will be for nothing if you forget your watch. Also, you can't count on a clock being at the testing site. Or the clock that is there may not be working.

11. Make sure to sharpen pencils the night before the exam. Buy No. 2 pencils and be sure to fill in the circle completely on the test. Partially-filled circles are counted as "omits" and count against you. In addition, any circles you leave blank will lower your score.

12. Carry your student ID with you to the test.

13. Do not clutter your testing area with backpacks, purses, or books. Leave such things at home.

14. Choose a seat at the test site that is near the front, in a corner. This position is advantageous because all distractions will be behind you. Also, you will get your test first and can be reading the written directions while others are waiting to get their exams.

15. Listen carefully to directions given by the proctor.

16. Because you have already decided how much time to spend on each question, be sure to stay with your plan if you are taking a timed test.

17. If you are taking your test on computer, be sure to raise your hand if you are having any problems.

18. Remember, you don't have to fear the test because
    A. you know there will be 40 questions;
    B. you know you have 45 minutes to complete the exam (if being timed);

C. you know you have prepared yourself through classroom activities and practice tests;
D. you know you have taken care of yourself physically;
E. you know you have taken care of yourself emotionally.

A CHECKLIST

A WEEK BEFORE THE TEST: (Date:_____)

_____1. Visit the building and room

_____2. Take medications prescribed by doctor regularly

_____3. Buy earplugs

_____4. Stop all substance abuse

TWO DAYS BEFORE THE TEST: (Date:_____)

_____1. Start getting adequate rest

_____2. Call parents or girl/boyfriend

_____3. Buy candy

_____4. Buy No 2. pencils

_____5. Buy or borrow a watch if you don't have one

ONE DAY BEFORE THE TEST: (Date:_____)

_____1. Pick out comfortable clothing

_____2. Stay to yourself. Don't let anyone upset you

_____3. Gather your ID, pencils, and watch

THE DAY OF THE TEST: (Date:_____)

_____ 1. Eat protein
_____ 2. Put on your watch
_____ 3. Carry ID, pencils, and candy in your pocket

CHAPTER TWO: GRAMMAR

Grammar is a system of rules by which sentences clearly deliver their meanings to the reader. By following these rules, you learn and understand how words are arranged into structures that are meaningful in the English language. The order of words in a sentence generally determines the meaning or message you want to convey. Therefore, if the arrangement of words is not consistent with conventional grammatical structure, you might convey a totally different message from the message you intended. In this chapter you we will cover typical grammar errors sometimes made by college students:

1) the Sentence Fragment
2) the Comma Splice
3) the Run-on Sentence
4) Verb Form Errors
5) Subject-Verb Agreement Errors
6) Pronoun Reference Errors

You will encounter errors such as these on Georgia English Exit Exams and be asked to correct them, so it is a good idea to practice the exercises until you understand the concepts well.

1. THE SENTENCE FRAGMENT

The sentence fragment is actually just that--a fragment (a part or portion of something). Thus, a sentence fragment is not an actual sentence but only a partial or incomplete one, generally because it lacks a subject or verb. Fragments are often phrases or subordinate clauses that can easily be corrected in two ways. The first correction technique is to add a subject or verb.

NOT THIS: *First on the floor and then on the table.*
BUT THIS: First on the floor and then on the table, *Ron danced* the night away.

The second strategy is to connect the fragment to an adjoining sentence as in

NOT THIS: *Which relaxes and rejuvenates him.*
BUT THIS: *Zac enjoys dining and dancing* which relaxes and rejuvenates him.

> Notice that the sentences are only complete when a subject and verb are added. Don't punctuate phrases or subordinate clauses as sentences. Just because a group of words starts with a capital letter and ends with a period does not necessarily mean that the group is a sentence.

Arthur and Pulley — Page 12

Exercise 1a. Complete the following constructions by adding a subject and/or verb.

1. Not coming in until very early the next morning.

2. With the cost of tuition steadily increasing.

3. The airplane with a ten-million-pound capacity.

4. Danced and danced for two solid hours.

5. Saw Enrique and was scared to death!

Exercise 1b. Complete the following constructions by adding the fragment to an existing independent clause.

6. Although Mr. Urteaga is a fine gentleman and close friend. He is untrustworthy in his relationships with women.

7. Why do heathens clamor? And fools rage?

8. Anita actually fell down and cried. Right in the middle of her argument with Liberace!

9. When I grow up and become a big boy. I want to be a football star.

10. Suzanna and Fabian are always fighting over who wears the most expensive clothes. Especially when they find themselves at the same parties.

Exercise 1c. Identify which of the following are fragments (f) and which are complete sentences (s).

11. ___ Because John and Twanna had been dating for years, their friends thought the two should marry.

12. ___ Where in the world did I lose my wallet and my picture of Leo?

13. ___ If I could go to church this morning.

14. ___ Because he hates talking about birds and bees.

15. ___ Although some individuals are taught not have sex before being blessed by the church.

16. ___ Elvira walked out the door, leaving Clarence extremely disappointed and heartbroken.

17. ___ And never returned to her home state.

18. ___ According to the gossip on the street, Hubert just won the lottery.

19. ___ Washington, DC is home to many African Americans who descended from tribes of southeast Africa.

20. ___ When children watch violent acts.

2. THE COMMA SPLICE

A comma splice exists when a comma is placed incorrectly between two complete sentences. A comma is not strong enough to separate entire sentences because it merely signals a pause within a thought. A complete sentence, on the other hand, suggests the end of an idea and is finalized by a period. The sentences below illustrate that the comma is not strong enough to separate the two "independent thoughts" presented.

NOT THIS: Sexual harassment is a big issue on campus for *women, men* are often harassed as well.

Charlotte failed English last *semester, she* has to enroll in the same course again.

One way in which a comma-splice error can be remedied is by replacing the comma with a period and beginning the next sentence with a capital letter, as shown here.

BUT THIS: Sexual harassment is a big issue on campus for *women. Men* are often harassed as well.

Charlotte failed English last *semester. She* has to enroll in the same course again.

Note: the length of a sentence has nothing to do with comma usage.

A comma splice can also be corrected by removing the comma and adding a semicolon in its place:

>Sexual harassment is a big issue on *campus; men* are often harassed as well.

>Charlotte failed English last *semester; she* has to enroll in the same course again.

Lastly, comma splice errors can be fixed by adding an appropriate coordinating conjunction after the comma, depending on the tone and logic of the sentence. Notice how the same sentences above are corrected by adding a comma and one of the FANBOYS (coordinating conjunctions) below:

COORDINATING CONJUNCTIONS (FANBOYS)

(f)	for
(a)	and
(n)	nor
(b)	but
(o)	or
(y)	yet
(s)	so

>Sexual harassment is a big issue on campus for women, *but* men are often harassed as well.

>Charlotte failed English last semester, *so* she has to enroll in the same course again.

Exercise 2a. Using a period, correct the comma splices in the following sentences.

1. Ali made all A's this semester, Kel made all F's except for the B he made in English.

2. I want true happiness when I grow up, I will need money, power, and fame.

3. Phillipe and Geneve were really happy together, they had no money, no power, and no fame.

Arthur and Pulley

4. Some people look for joy from without, others find their joy from within.

5. Anna Kay is an exceptional grandmother, she guards here grandchildren with her life.

6. Damascus is a mystical town, it's the birthplace of many spiritual leaders.

7. Understanding and compassion are such positive, powerful qualities, what a wonderfully different world we would live in if more of us possessed them.

8. Sometimes the road ahead seems long and winding, other times it seems short and straight.

9. Can you come and take me away to a place under the sun, will you be around when I need you?

10. Florian and Isabeau lived a life devoted to others, I wonder if they were ever rewarded.

Exercise 2b. Now correct these comma splice errors by using the semicolon.

1. Some say beauty is only skin deep, I say it goes deeper than that.

2. African-Americans are beautiful, Whites, Asians, and Latins are too.

3. The dinner was delicious, the conversation was stimulating.

4. Come with me on a far away journey, I will make you happy forever.

5. Underline or italicize titles of books, put witty sayings inside quotation marks.

6. This present life seems hard to bear sometimes, I wonder if there is an afterlife that will be euphoric.

7. Mr. Morganstern left his home and family for Tokyo some years ago, he never came back.

8. Nobody wants to babysit Jada and Jayson, they're very naughty children.

9. Mr. Pulley's son, Tristan, is a wonderful young man, he excels in everything he does.

10. The stars are bright tonight, romance is in the air.

Exercise 2c. **Correct the following comma splice errors in the sentences below by using the most logical FANBOY.**

1. Cora Sue made a delicious apple crumb cobbler, her husband ate it all in thirty minutes.

2. Pierre and his girlfriend were totally in love during the first few weeks of their relationship, after two months it was all over between them.

3. Jed, Clarence, and Maple all live together, they can't stand the sight of each other.

4. Come to me if you are tired and weary, I will give you a quiet place to rest.

5. I really need an A in this class, I hope I pass the next test.

6. We can't keep driving on empty, we're going to be stranded in the dark very soon.

7. Jedidiah decided to leave Joellen to go to Australia with Eric, Jedidiah is not sure if he made the right decision.

8. Many cooks today can't stand the heat, they need to get out of the kitchen.

9. I saw Bubba steal money from the cash register, the store manager saw Bubba giving the money away to a homeless woman.

10. The tired and weary mountain climbers decided not to ever go again, the first trip was a horrible experience.

3. THE RUN-ON SENTENCE

A run-on sentence exists when two or more complete thoughts or sentences have no signal of pause (comma), no stop (period or semicolon), nor coordinating conjunction (FANBOY). All the ideas run together, making the ideas difficult to comprehend.

NOT THIS: Drinking and driving is a deadly combination people don't really consider the consequences and they drink and drive anyway.

It was pouring rain Wilma and Kathleen went to sunbathe on the beach.

Arthur and Pulley

Correct a run-on sentence by breaking it into complete sentences and punctuating it appropriately. In most cases, you will have to add a coordinating conjunction (FANBOY).

BUT THIS: Drinking and driving is a deadly *combination, but* people drink and drive *anyway. P*eople don't really consider the consequences.

It was pouring *rain, but* Wilma and Kathleen went to sunbathe on the beach anyway.

Exercise 3a. Correct the following run-on sentences.

1. My date dropped me off at home only to pick up another girl later I sat alone and cried bitterly.

2. Come to my house on the lake we can have a very good time watching the turtles bathe.

3. Carlita passed her entrance exams with flying colors this semester last year she had failed by one point.

4. Some say there is a Supreme Being that can make the earth tremble and shake others say it's all a matter of science.

5. It's important to know what you believe it's also important to know why you believe it.

6. My car kept swerving to the right and left in the drenching rain I almost lost control and crashed.

7. I wish Marlinda Ann would come home from the square dance John needs help lifting the calf from the porch.

8. We had an interesting lesson on the pros and cons of dating I still fell asleep.

9. The Clampits went to Egypt last summer they said that they may go to Paris this year.

10. Fools rage evil people destroy!

Mastery Exercise. Identify the comma splices (CS) and run-on sentences (R-O) in the following constructions. Then, correct the error.

_____1. Fabio and Giovanni played basketball all day long, they went to evening church service at 7:00 p.m.

_____2. Scarlet lied about having a date with Melanie's husband, the two women still remained good friends.

_____3. I tried to find a convenient place to park at the rave he said there was parking available on the back lot only.

_____4. Earlier in the day I had wanted to party and dance, my boyfriend changed my mind.

_____5. What can I say I have no explanation for my behavior I'm just a fool in love!

_____6. It's really interesting the way Ebony and Ivory say they love each other more than life itself they fight and argue all the time.

_____7. Let's get together for dinner tomorrow evening, I want to get your opinion on something.

_____8. When my great grandfather considered that half his life was spent in a dark world he wanted to die then his friends talked him out of taking drastic measures.

_____9. Next summer I refuse to work, I will go to far away lands as my friend Linda does each year.

_____10. I wish I could get out of this place, the flourescent lights are making me dizzy.

4. VERB ERRORS

Verb Forms. Verbs have at least three main parts. They are the simple present form (as in *fly*), the simple past form (as in *flew*), and the past participle form (as in *flown*). The present participle form (as in *flying*) is sometimes considered a fourth part. These principal parts include regular and irregular verbs, as in the sampling below:

PRESENT:	PAST:	PAST PARTICPLE:
arise	arose	arisen
ask	asked	asked
awaken	awakened	awakened
bear	bore	borne/born
bring	brought	brought
choose	chose	chosen
dive	dived/dove	dived
draw	drew	drawn
drown	drowned	drowned
fly	flew	flown
freeze	froze	frozen
hang (things)	hung	hung
hang (people)	hanged	hanged
shrink	shrank/shrunk	shrunk/shrunken
spring	sprang/sprung	sprung
strive	strove/strived	striven/strived
swing	swung	swung
throw	threw	thrown

Present: I *ask* for water, but I get Coke.
Past: I *asked* for water, but I got Coke.
Past Participle (using *has, had, have*): I had *asked* for water, but I got Coke.

Present: I *strive* to overcome my smoking habit.
Past: I *strove/strived* to overcome my smoking habit for two years.
Past Participle (using *has, had, have*): I have *striven/strived* to overcome my smoking habit.

Exercise 4a. Complete the following sentences by supplying the appropriate verb form:

1. The wind is_____so hard today. (*blow*)

2. Oh, my gosh, the children have really_____in the lake! (*fall*)

3. Antonio is the one I would have_____for the position. (*choose*)

4. After I wash my clothes, I_____them on the porch to dry. (*hang*)

5. It was a really hot day, so Marlo _____ into the cool water. (dive)

6. I was surprised to see that my blouse had _____ after only two dry cleanings. (shrink)

7. Like a miracle, unexpectedly, Mariah _____ from her bed of affliction and walked. (arise)

8. After we got home from our road trip, we _____ our clothes and food inside from the car. (bring)

9. The entire month of January the ground was _____. (freeze)

10. Scots have _____ (throw) pebbles across Loch Ness for centuries.

Verb Tense: Verbs change form to express that an action occurred in the present, the past, or the future. Generally, we recognize six tenses: three simple tenses and three perfect tenses. Usually, use of tense is consistent throughout a sentence, a paragraph, or an essay, unless there is legitimate/logical reason for shifting (for instance, from present to past or vice-versa).

Simple Tenses:

Present

I often go to town to buy food and clothes.

Past

After eating and getting dressed, Sermo went dancing with Judy.

Future

After partying all night with my date, Jeremy will go home alone.

Perfect Tenses:

Present Perfect

Mike and Steve have partied since we saw each other last week.

Past Perfect

Catie and Daniel had danced until dawn.

Future Perfect

Harriet and Jacqueline will have eaten and gotten dressed before midnight.

Exercise 4b. Write a sentence for each of the six tenses.

1._____

2._____

3._____

4._____

5._____

6._____

5. SUBJECT-VERB AGREEMENT

Verbs must agree with their subjects. If a subject is plural, the verb must have a plural form, and if the subject is singular, the verb must have a singular form.

SINGULAR:	The *boy* in the pool *is* wet.
PLURAL:	The *girls* in the barn, however, *are* warm and dry.

There are certain collective nouns and phrases that refer to a group of things or individuals as a singular unit. Consequently, whether they require a singular or a plural verb depends on whether the sentence refers to the group as a whole or to the individual items or persons within the group. Consider the following example:

The *committee is* coming to terms with its decision. (single unit/single verb)

The *faculty members are* meeting to discuss salary proposals. (one group but many members/plural verb)

Five million *dollars is* a lot of money. (plural but regarded as one unit)

Exercise 5a. Supply the appropriate singular or plural verb to these constructions, making sure they agree with the subject.

1. Mario and Suazo, the boys next door, *(is/are)* truly the best of friends.

2. The group of tenants down the hallway *(is/are)* unaccepting of Jamie and Johnnie's living arrangement.

3. The choir *(was/were)* singing when the storm struck.

4. The students in the Spanish class brought all of their textbooks to class, but one of their textbooks *(was/were)* not used.

5. All the students in English class today *(was/were)* blinded by the tornado that swept through the classroom.

6. PRONOUN REFERENCE ERRORS

   Pronoun references should be immediately obvious. It should always be clear to what noun the pronoun refers.

   UNCLEAR: Jorge, Julio, and Juan were making dinner, and Julio wanted *him* to fry the tortillas.
   (To whom does *him* refer, Jorge or Juan? Who actually fried the tortillas?)

   CLEAR: Jorge, Julio, and Juan were making dinner, and Julio wanted *Juan* to fry the tortillas.

   UNCLEAR: Carlos told Shelton that *he* had made a mistake.
   (Who made the mistake, Carlos or Shelton?)

   CLEAR: *Carlos* admitted *his* mistake to Shelton.

Exercise 6a. Correct the unclear pronoun references in the following sentences:

1. Mary burned Sue's dinner until it was black, but *she* said she liked it that way.

2. After Peter, James, and John found the crown in the cellar, John looked at Peter and James and placed it on *his* head.

3. The Halloween mask clung tightly to Gerald's face, making *it* look even uglier than before.

4. As Kimiko and Fabio watched the tall oak trees sway in the wind, *they* fell to the ground.

5. Turenda told Annise that *she* could do anything she wanted to do.

Pronoun Antecedents. Pronouns have to agree with the nouns to which they refer in terms of gender and number. If the noun is male and singular, the pronoun must be male and singular. The following sentences represent this idea of agreement:

George saw *his (masculine singular pronoun)* hand fall off as the ax fell.

When she tripped on the ledge of the building while trying to reach the injured bird, *Marylou* fell to *her (feminine singular pronoun)* death.

All the *students* miserably failed *their (plural pronoun)* final exams.

Exercise 6b. Supply the appropriate pronouns in these sentences:

1. He didn't do his homework, but neither did his friend, Lily, do *theirs/hers*.

2. Every one of my children *is/are* afflicted with some kind of emotional conflict.

3. When a person tells others that *they have/he or she has* never lied, *they are/he is* lying through *their/his* teeth.

4. Each of us should have a job of *our/his or her* own.

5. Any woman who wants *their/her* nails polished should have *them/it* done by a manicurist who knows what *they are/he or she is* doing.

Now, correct any antecedent problems in the following sentences.

6. Everyone in the room has their books and supplies.

7. In all the chaos of the train derailment, no one was able to find their belongings.

8. Each girl, including Sue, will buy their own dress.

9. As the train hit the bus going across the tracks, it crashed.

10. Sometimes, when a person tells a lie, they feel guilty about the deed.

Name_____Date_____Score_____

MASTERY TEST ONE

Now see what you've learned about sentence fragments, comma splices, run-on sentences, verb forms, subject-verb agreement, tense, and pronoun reference and agreement.

A. Correct any fragments in the following sentences:

1. The door with the broken lock.

_____

2. Coming home from a night of wild partying.

_____

3. A big issue regarding world peace.

_____

4. When the students came to class without their assignments.

_____

5. If Carol and Sue have to enroll in the same course again.

_____

B. Eliminate the comma splices and insert appropriate punctuation (period, semicolon, or comma and coordinating conjunction) in the following sentences:

6. Chuck is a very exciting man, he can practically walk on water.

_____

7. Marissa and Hector really do love each other, they just can't live together.

_____

8. Why do fools rage and evil men destroy, why do leaders of nations imagine vain and foolish things?

_____

9. A little knowledge is a dangerous thing, no knowledge at all is deadly.

_____

10. The stars are not shining brightly tonight, it seems that clouds are darkening the skies.

_____

C. If any of the following sentences are run-on constructions, write "RO" in the space provided.

11. ____ My final exams were so hard to pass this semester I thought I would fail both English and math.

Arthur and Pulley

12. ____ Why did the babysitter leave before we returned home didn't he know we would be furious?

13. ____ The housing projects became a very dangerous place to live, so my family and I moved to Beverly Hills.

14. ____ I hate to eat spinach because it tastes so awful.

15. ____ Listening to classical music used to be my favorite hobby now I enjoy playing soccer more than anything else.

D. *Correct any verb form, subject-verb agreement, or tense error in these sentences.*

16. _____ If Sheila could have gone to the prom with anyone she wanted, she would have *chose* Stephen as her date.

17. _____ Each of the young men *are* very good looking.

18. _____ I often go to the grocery store and *bought* bread, tomatoes, and milk.

19. _____ Did the snow *fell* all evening long?

20. _____ The team members *was* trying hard to win the game, but the competition was just too tough.

E. *Make the pronoun references clear and clarify any pronoun number, gender, and antecedent problems in the sentences below.*

21. Margaret Ann, Sue Ellen, and Billy Bob were all dancing and having a good time when Billy Bob announced that he wanted her to leave the party and go home immediately.

_____

22. Herbert told Chris that he did not belong in a place like that.

_____

Arthur and Pulley

23. Not one student brought their books to class.

_____

24. Each of us has their own hardships in this life.

_____

25. As Ian and Paddy looked up at the planets, it seemed as if they would fall to the ground.

_____

CHAPTER THREE : PUNCTUATION

Punctuation is the practice or system of using accepted standardized marks in writing to clarify the meanings of sentences. That is, in written text, punctuation is used to help the reader know when to pause so that the material is understandable. For example, what would happen in the reader's mind if he or she encountered something like:

Roger is more than just a rude person who is inconsiderate of females being in a position of power he lords over women making their working life miserable not only does Roger cause them to feel unworthy to be in his presence but he also causes them to feel uneasy in actuality Roger is the one who is in need of psychological counseling it seems he is the one who has issues with feeling insecure and small.

Although a reader could eventually figure out the meaning of the sentence structures above, it would have been much easier to comprehend had the writer inserted punctuation marks:

Roger is more than just a rude person who is inconsiderate of females. Being in a position of power, he lords over women. Making their working life miserable, not only does Roger cause them to feel unworthy to be in his presence, but he also causes them to feel uneasy. In actuality, Roger is the one who is in need of psychological counseling. It seems he is the one who has issues with feeling insecure and small.

Three of the most often-used punctuation marks are the comma, semicolon, and colon. We discuss each of them in this chapter. In addition, information on how to use the apostrophe is presented.

THE COMMA

Comma use is extremely important in writing because when the comma is placed incorrectly, the entire meaning/message of an idea can be lost. Conversely, when commas are placed systematically and strategically (correctly), meanings and ideas are very clear and understandable. Most commonly, the comma is used for three reasons:

    1) to separate items in a series,
    2) to link independent clauses using a coordinating conjunction (FANBOY), and
    3) to follow introductory words, phrases, and clauses.

Note the following example of commas used in *items in a series*:

The only items that Pablo needed to take on his Jamaican cruise were shoes, shorts, tee shirts, and money.

Exercise 1a. Now, place commas correctly in the sentences containing items in a series.

1. De'Andre's last will and testament stipulated that upon his death his brother would receive De'Andre's money jewelry book collection and antique alarm clock.

2. Jeff was surprised to learn that Mohammed's favorite leisure-time activities were skydiving bungee jumping sailing and skiing.

3. Hal and Jada are angry with their preacher because the reverend drinks and curses.

4. Eloise's best friends are Joline Kristin Lamont Malek and Henry.

5. The Fuqua family lost everything they owned in the fire, including an awarding-winning stamp collection a set of heirloom china and a handcrafted bookcase.

6. Helio feels that he could be a happier person if he had more money owned more property and gave more to charitable organizations.

7. Some people are considered insensitive simply because they do not cry at funerals and weddings help older people to cross the street laugh at others' jokes or give words of comfort to the downtrodden.

8. It's not nice to make a fool of Mother Nature Mother Teresa and Father Time.

9. It's hard to decide whether to travel by airplane bus or go-cart because these means of transportation are easily accessible.

10. Why can't we all just get along as friends neighbors and fellow citizens?

Consider the following example of comma use to link independent clauses (by using a coordinating conjunction). Remember, coordinating conjunctions [FANBOYS] connect two independent clauses.

I want to visit Paris one day, *but* I'm afraid to fly.

Exercise 1b. *Now, underline the FANBOYS, and then place commas appropriately in the following sentences.*

1. Many people talk of living in eternal peace, <u>but</u> none of them seems to want to die first.

2. Randy went bowling last night instead of studying, <u>so</u> he made an "F" on his math test.

3. Get in the house right now <u>or</u> you will suffer great consequences!

4. Paula dyed her hair purple last night, <u>and</u> she permed it this morning.

5. Genova decided to go back to college and earn a degree, <u>for</u> she knew that waiting tables was not what she wanted to do for the rest of her life.

6. I once thought that I wanted to marry Melinda, <u>but</u> now I don't want to marry anyone.

7. Henrietta had meant to leave Steve's house at midnight, <u>but</u> he decided that she should stay until 6:00 a.m. <u>so</u> that she wouldn't have to drive late at night.

8. Some people don't like to just stay at home watching television for pleasure, <u>nor</u> do they find enjoyment in taking strolls in the park.

9. Some students study for hours each day, <u>yet</u> they often fail their courses.

10. Get busy mowing the lawn and cleaning the garage, <u>or</u> you will not go to the dance tonight!

Consider these examples of using a comma to follow introductory words or phrases.

Yes, I'd be happy to accompany you to the masked ball on Halloween night.
When you walk through a storm, hold your head up high.

Exercise 1c. Place commas correctly in these sentences that use introductory words and phrases.

1. Really you need to "get a life" and stop meddling in mine.

2. While Anastasio and Merlin were in the backyard cooking out together the doorbell rang.

3. No we won't be available until the "Twelfth of Never!"

4. If I lost ten pounds or fifty pounds would anyone notice?

5. Yes Martin and Josephine would actually go to Europe if you paid their airfare.

6. Because you don't work hard at passing your classes you won't pass them.

7. As the soldiers raised the American flag the crowd gathered in silence.

8. Somehow I really don't think Anna will do well in chemistry.

9. No do not e-mail me any information about what happened on your last date.

10. Every time that Judd visits Manuel's home Manuel shuts the door in Judd's face.

Exercise 1d. Identify where commas should be placed in the following sentences:

1. When I get up in the morning I like to wash my face eat breakfast get dressed walk the dog and smoke before I go to work.
   (LOCATE AND MARK TWO COMMON COMMA USES)

2. Although adults assume that teenagers never engage in sexual activity before marriage they hope that teens will use protection.
   (LOCATE AND MARK ONE COMMON COMMA USE)

3. Yes one of my friends used to take drugs every day but he changed his behavior months ago because he realized it was detrimental to his well-being.
   (LOCATE AND MARK TWO COMMON COMMA USES)

4. Teri made a vow to pass her marine biology class yet she hasn't made any real effort to do any assignments.
   (LOCATE AND MARK ONE COMMON COMMA USE)

5. Because I go to church and pray every day my mama says that I have a special place in Heaven.
(LOCATE AND MARK ONE COMMON COMMA USE)

6. Marlow couldn't possibly consider himself dressed because he's still missing his pants socks and shoes.
(LOCATE AND MARK ONE COMMON COMMA USE)

7. Shemika failed to pick up the hammer nails screwdriver and pocket knife.
(LOCATE AND MARK ONE COMMON COMMA USE)

8. Please get all of the animals out of the house especially the dog cat monkey and tiger.
(LOCATE AND MARK TWO COMMON COMMA USES)

9. If Brandy and Steve could only get to know each other better I'm sure they would make a fine couple.
(LOCATE AND MARK ONE COMMON COMMA USE)

10. When Horst and Enrique announced their resignations from the university no one even cared enough to ask them why.
(LOCATE AND MARK ONE COMMON COMMA USE)

THE SEMICOLON

You may have been taught previously that the semicolon is often used interchangeably with the period to separate two independent clauses, but the rules really are not that simple. There are two elements that must be present when the semicolon is the punctuation of choice. First, the two sentences must be very closely related in idea; second, the two clauses must be relatively short. Otherwise, a period is more suitable. Another use of the semicolon is to separate sentence elements that contain internal commas.

Consider the following examples:

Ronny walked fast; Colleen just took her time.

Listening to dull, uninteresting, boring *lectures;* walking down lonely, deserted, dark *streets;* and just sitting and watching the grass grow, ducks swim in ponds, and children romp about are my favorite things to do.

The dinner was *great;* the conversation was even better.

4. Never would I have thought that driving a dull, boring, uneventful back road at 100 miles per *hour;* letting the cold, damp, hard wind blow through my hair; and staring straight ahead into an empty, deserted path could be such an exhilarating experience.

Exercise 2a. Now, try constructing sentences of your own that make use of the above semicolon applications:

1. _____
2. _____
3. _____
4. _____
5. _____

Exercise 2b. Practice what you have learned by identifying which of the following sentences are punctuated correctly (yes) or incorrectly (no). If the sentence is not punctuated correctly, insert commas and/or semicolons where they should be.

1. ___ Harriet is an intelligent, gorgeous, vivacious woman; her sister is even more beautiful.

2. ___ Gustavo is from Venezuela, his stepbrother is from Colombia.

3. ___ He looked right through me as if I weren't there; I never meant to hurt him.

4. ___ Even though I've had many good experiences, life remains essentially a mystery to me.

5. ___ Pessimists think that life is actually a bowl of cherries a batch gone bad.

6. ___ A long walk through the park a tall glass of cold tea a moonlight serenade or a drive in the country makes everything good in my world.

7. ___ The boys in that group are tall, dark, handsome, and ambitious; the girls are gorgeous, classy, and intelligent.

8. ___ Jermaine may have passed his English exam but he cheated by copying from his notes.

9. ___ If I were you, I'd pack my raincoat, boots, scarf, and gloves; it's very cold outside and looks like it's going to rain.

10. ___ No I can't go I have too much to do.

11. ___ Lying in a warm cozy bed sipping a cool refreshing glass of lemonade and watching my favorite suspenseful captivating movies is all I think about during the summer.

12. ___ I can't make the trip to the mall or the grocery store, for I have too much homework to do.

13. ___ My mother thinks I'm crazy, my daddy thinks I'm cute.

14. ___ When Samora is in a bad mood, she usually goes on long, all-day shopping sprees; cuts her tall, overgrown grass; and washes her dirty, hard-to-reach windows.

15. ___ Because you have been honest with me I respect you more than ever.

THE COLON

Most commonly, the colon calls attention to what follows, such as an explanation, a summary, or a listing (items in a series) as in the following examples:

Jeremy's sorrow was laced with *depression: every night he cried himself to sleep after looking at a photo of his ex-girlfriend.*

Surprisingly enough, my first impression of him was the same as that of my last *boyfriend: tall, dark, strikingly handsome, kind, and generous.*

When Michael went to the Bahamas, he brought back the following *items: sunglasses, suntan lotion, goggles, swim trunks, and a new life partner.*

Exercise 3a. Place colons correctly in the following sentences*:*

1. The street was rampant with elements of violence and crime guns, knives, swords, anger, hostility, and bitterness.

2. The applicant lacks an essential quality intelligence.

3. Several family members will not be invited to the reunion this year Denyce, Mykel, Jayson, and Sula.

4. LaWanda has such a joyful spirit she constantly sings and smiles.

5. The Admissions Office requested a number of materials, including the following items high school transcript, health report, letters of recommendation, and test scores.

6. How can anyone have as hateful a personality as Juan mean, bitter, hostile, brutal?

7. Marissa needed to pick up the following items from the store bread, milk, cheese, butter, and rice.

8. Bryan bought nearly all of his school supplies except these pens, crayons, and book markers.

9. My boyfriend has great attributes that I admire intelligence, generosity, kindness, and a sense of humor.

10. Monrovia will never have a happy, fulfilled life she is a mean and hateful girl.

THE APOSTROPHE

The apostrophe serves three major functions in effective written communication.
    1) It forms the possessive of nouns;
    2) it symbolizes one or more omitted letters; and
    3) it forms the plurals of letters and numerals.

> The apostrophe does not, however, form plurals of nouns nor the possessive case of personal pronouns (e.g., cows, males, universities, theirs, its, hers, his).

1. *Possessive Nouns*

   A. The possessive case of nouns serves to communicate ownership or close relationship. Note the following examples of the apostrophe used to form the possessive of nouns:

      a. (ownership)   the *boy's* dog
                                  Mina's white shirt

b. (close relationship) the *book's* theme
the *story's* meaning

B. In addition to nouns, some indefinite pronouns serve to communicate possession. (An indefinite pronoun makes reference to non-specific persons or things, for instance, as in *no one* or *someone*.) Consider the following examples:

a. The burning trash in the garage was really *no one's* fault.
b. *Someone's* coat was accidentally damaged at the prom.

C. Use an apostrophe to show possession when a singular noun ends in *s*, as in the following examples:

a. *Kris's* benevolent attitude will take her far in life.
b. All the *business's* clients decided to take their concerns to an attorney.

D. When a plural noun ends in *s*, the apostrophe is placed after the *s*, as in these examples:

a. The *teachers'* maternity leaves are over.
b. Some of the *employees'* contracts will be renewed.

E. When a plural noun doesn't end in *s*, add the apostrophe, then the *s*, as in these examples:

a. The *men's* bathroom is especially nice and clean smelling, today.
b. Conversely, the *women's* bathroom could use a good sterilization treatment.

Exercise 4a. Place apostrophes correctly in the following sentences.

1. How can you say that this is not (anyone) backpack?

2. (Eddie) car is such a horrible looking vehicle.

3. Many of the (students) papers were handed in on time.

4. The (novel) plot was nothing like I thought it would be.

5. Not only are the (women) futures at stake here but the (children) as well.

6. Is this the (men) or (women) locker room?

7. Are the Harry Potter books adult literature or (children) literature?

8. (Alyss) parents were born in Lancaster, England.

9. The tribal (leaders) discussion was not popular with the women.

10. Never knock on (anyone) door unless you know the person who lives in the house.

11. Every time we visit Sweden, (somebody) souvenirs are lost in the crowds.

12. All of the pretty potted plants are (their).

13. Tom didn't know whether the textbooks were left at his (friend) house or at two different (neighbor) houses.

14. Several of the (boy) coats were scorched by the cleaning fluid.

15. One (girl) dress was completely destroyed.

2. The apostrophe frequently stands in for omitted letters or words in contractions (words from which one or more letters have been deliberately omitted and in which apostrophes are used to indicate the omission). Although contractions may render the sentence a little less formal, they are frequently used in writing. The following is a list of some commonly used contractions:

aren't	*meaning*	are not	she's	*meaning*	she is or has
can't	*meaning*	cannot	there's	*meaning*	there is
didn't	*meaning*	did not	they're	*meaning*	they are
don't	*meaning*	do not	wasn't	*meaning*	was not
he's	*meaning*	he is or has	we're	*meaning*	we are
it's	*meaning*	it is	weren't	*meaning*	were not
I'd	*meaning*	I would or I had	we've	*meaning*	we have
I'm	*meaning*	I am	who's	*meaning*	who is
isn't	*meaning*	is not	won't	*meaning*	will not
let's	*meaning*	let us	you're	*meaning*	you are

Exercise 4b. Supply contractions where appropriate, or if contractions are given, write their meanings.

1. He is not playing fairly.

2. Tom and Eddie were not forced out of town; they left willingly.

3. If I'd known you were planning to go skating, I'd have gone, too.

4. She's a fool if she thinks I'm going to believe her husband's lies!

5. No, I can't tolerate such rude behavior; he's just totally out of order.

6. You are so special to me and to so many others.

7. Why we can't marry and live happily forever is a mystery to me.

8. I am so crazy about you!

9. She's willing to go to Europe this fall, but her boyfriend is reluctant because he's been afraid to fly ever since he was a child.

10. Life seems most difficult when you're trying to do the right thing.

3. Plurals

   A. Use apostrophes for forming plurals of letters, numbers, and words used as terms. Note that two styles are acceptable when forming the plural of years—with or without the apostrophe—as in *1990's* or *1990s.*

   a. The *P's* in Jeff's essay are poorly formed.

   b. I can't make out this address; there appears to be, however, three *5's* in the house number.

   c. The author of this text seems to have made some serious errors; all the *to's* are spelled as *two's.*

Exercise 4c. Using the above patterns, place apostrophes correctly in the following sentences.

1. The Japanese third graders had trouble writing 7s but no problem pronouncing 7s in their native tongue.

2. It's hard to read this map because all the area markings look like 8s and 9s.

3. Jon, can you make your Rs a little more clear?

4. When Mikya and Margaret studied their multiplication tables in elementary school, they had more trouble learning their 4s than their 6s.

5. Mrs. Ricardo keeps confusing her *theirs* with her *there's* every time she writes a letter.

6. During the 1960s and 1970s, students at Berkeley gathered to protest the Vietnam War.

7. It must have been interesting to watch men parading in dresses in the late 1700s.

8. Terry's Vs look so much like Us that it is hard to get the message of his sentences.

9. Most history Ph.D.s are still looking for desirable positions, while M.A.s have all but given up hope of finding a good job.

10. Shartica's Is are not legible; consequently, her *tins* appear to be *tens*.

AVOID MISUSE OF THE APOSTROPHE!

1. Don't use the apostrophe with the present tense verb form:

   INCORRECT: Tyrone lives' a very exciting life in Mayberry, North Carolina.

2. Don't use the apostrophe at the end of a non-possessive noun ending in *s:*

   INCORRECT: Culture studies' reveal that most North Carolinians are much happier people than Midwesterners.

3. Don't use an apostrophe to form a non-possessive plural:

   INCORRECT: Many children's don't even care about making A's in school.

Exercise 4d. Now, rewrite the above sentences correctly on the lines below:

1. _____

2. _____

3. _____

Name_____ Date_____ Score_____

MASTERY TEST TWO

Write "yes" before sentences that are punctuated correctly. Write "no" before sentences punctuated incorrectly, and then punctuate the sentence correctly.

1. ___ Luke's worst mistake was that he stopped running looked around and fell to the ground.

2. ___ When a victim doesn't want to testify the judge won't make him.

3. ___ Grandma taught me well I never cross the street without looking both ways first.

4. ___ It was difficult for Wilma to choose her preferred means of transportation because there were so many choices including the following airplane car boat and bus.

5. ___ Low interest rates make this a good time to buy houses cars jewelry and land.

6. ___ Long, hot, summer days; old, worn-out cars; irresponsible, trifling adults; and heartless, cold-blooded people all really get on my nerves.

7. ___ If you don't want fleas, don't lie down with dogs.

8. ___ When they were in high school Jennifer and Eloise were called "bookworms" and "nerds" Jesse and Randall were called "geeks" and "sissies."

9. ___ When you're having a bad day, try talking to Lillie Mae; she cares.

10. ___ Today is not your day tomorrow doesn't look good either

11. ___ Pray for love and peace; prepare for the unknown.

12. ___ Sure we can party all night.

13. ___ If at first you don't succeed try harder next time.

14. ___ Somehow we survive each day in a world of sex drugs and violence.

15. ___ The following description of the bank robber should help police to find their man: male, age 40, 6ft, 280lbs, brown hair, green eyes, and a large ugly scar on his left cheek.

16. ___ Carmen told Homer that she would date him when the following conditions were met hell had frozen over donkeys had flown over the moon and there had been sixteen inches of snow in July.

17. ___ Shut up and drive we're going to be late.

18. ___ A good car may is hard to find; at the very least, a buyer must have the following inspected: alternator, transmission, tires, and starter.

19. ___ What did you see when you visited Orlando Atlanta Savannah and Goose Creek?

20. ___ Tommy Graves wasn't his real name everything he told us was a lie.

21. ___ For breakfast I like bacon eggs ham cheese and milk.

22. ___ I love individuals who are nice and smart but I don't like being around individuals who are rude and unintelligent.

23. ___ Because all people are not the same size, department stores sell clothing in sizes small, medium, large, and extra large.

24. ___ Some people have it all looks talent fame fortune personality.

25. ___ If you're not satisfied with our product ask for your money back you'll get it right away.

26. ___ She lacks only one thing that I look for in a relationship an ability to laugh at herself.

27. ___ Mr. Gratersen isn't really quite as nasty as I thought he was: people say he gives food to the hungry.

28. ___ My parents are always saying that there are a lot of "crazies" out there, so you can never be too careful.

29. ___ Will you have dinner with me if I prepare these dishes: sauerkraut, turnip greens, apple cobbler, and pigs' feet?

30. ___ I dont work for these reasons lack of ambition plenty of money and an aunt who taught me the value of relaxing.

31. ___When it rains it pours.

32. ___Why is it always raining cats and dogs not pigs' and goats'?

33. ___My best friend just returned from studying abroad in Italy and I was amazed at how enthusiastic she was about her experience.

34. ___Yes Carlos and Mr. Martinez are the guilty culprits they should be sentenced to death.

35. ___If students could pass all of their courses with "B" grades their chances of getting college scholarships would increase, they would feel a sense of accomplishment in themselves and they would have happy proud and boastful parents.

36. ___What do you mean by saying shes nothing but a secretary?

37. ___My brains functions are all but dead.

38. ___Dont walk so fast; the childrens little legs can't keep up with us.

39. ___Could we not go to the farmers plantation tomorrow when it's not so hot outside?

40. ___Lydia and Antonio were both born in the 1930s.

41. ___Sara's greatest misfortune occurred because she had no money fame nor power.

42. ___If you don't want to be nervous and anxious about the writing test, get some sleep and eat a hearty breakfast.

43. ___I enjoy classical and rock music but I don't like rhythm and blues or jazz.

44. ___Some of us seem to be so down on our luck no job no home no family no friends.

45. ___If you fall from the horse get up and try to mount it again.

46. ___When teachers learn that students have many courses they will be more lenient.

47. ___No Sylvester and Allen did not commit the crime they should not be sent to prison.

48. ___Peter said that he would die if his girlfriend broke up with him he did die fifty years later.

49. ___School is finally out, so let's throw a party and have lots of fun.

50. ___Of all the seasons of the year I like fall the best.

CHAPTER FOUR: SENTENCE STRUCTURE

Sentence structure refers to the pattern of a group of words that makes a complete thought (sentence). To eliminate confusion of ideas, sentences are put together in a certain order. Sentences should be constructed clearly and logically to avoid misinterpretation by your readers. Some common sentence errors that obstruct clarity are misplaced and dangling modifiers, faulty parallelism, mixed constructions, and word order errors.

MISPLACED MODIFIERS

A modifier is a word or phrase that describes another word or phrase. The location of the modifier in the sentence often determines the sentence's meaning; consequently, its proper placement is determined by the message you want to express. If a word or phrase is misplaced, it can actually change the meaning you are trying to convey and, at times, the sentence simply sounds strange. To avoid making errors, place the modifier beside the word or phrase it modifies. Notice the following examples:

He *merely* said that she was just a child.
(He slightly or casually said that she was a child.)

He said that she was *merely a child.*
(He said that she was simply or just a child.)

***Only* teachers like to go to school on weekends.**
(Teachers are the only ones who like to go to school on weekends.)

Teachers say that they *only* like to go to school on weekends.)
(Teachers don't like to go to school on week days.)

NOT THIS: ***Coming down hard and fast,* the students just stood there watching the rain.**
   (Were the *students* or was *the rain* coming down hard and fast?)

BUT THIS: **The students just stood there watching the rain *coming down hard and fast.***
   (Notice that *coming down hard and fast* now correctly modifies rain.)

NOT THIS: **The guy that she thought would make her happy *totally* drove her crazy.**
   (Was she expecting to be *totally happy*, or was she *totally crazy*? Shouldn't *totally* modify happy? As it stands, totally is modifying *crazy*.)

Arthur and Pulley Page 46

BUT THIS: The guy that she thought would make her *totally* happy drove her crazy.

Exercise 1a. Correct the misplaced modifiers in the following sentences. In some cases, the modifier may appear in two different places in a sentence, and either placement is correct:

1. Miss Martin watched the stars standing on a hill.
   _____

2. The highway was jammed with traffic during the holidays, not surprisingly.
   _____

3. I am tired tonight, especially.
   _____

4. Time will tell only whether Jim and Suellyn will rekindle their friendship.
   _____

5. The charge for the drapes and the kitchen appliances just is included in the cost of the house.
   _____

6. Football coaches earn more money than drama coaches on the average.
   _____

7. Marissa refused to marry Maurice after she learned of his affairs, obviously.
   _____

8. David and Roger talked with their dead wives with their eyes tightly closed.

_____

9. Women live longer lives than men generally.

_____

10. The food in the dining room is just for the guests and their dates.

_____

DANGLING MODIFIERS

A dangling modifier is a word or phrase that cannot logically describe any word or phrase in a sentence. That is, you have written a modifier or describer, but you have left out the word or phrase it modifies; therefore, it "dangles" all by itself. When the word or phrase that is supposed to be modified is left out of the sentence, your modifier "is lost" as in the following sentence:

NOT THIS: Many happy times can be experienced *doing random acts of kindness for others.*

Doing random acts of kindness for others is a dangling modifier. It seems to modify *happy times*, but this idea makes no sense—"happy times" can't "do random acts." The word which is left out is "people," or a word like "people." People can do random acts of kindness.

You can correct dangling modifiers in one of two ways. 1) One way to clarify the idea of this sentence is to add a word or group of words that the modifier can logically modify as in this sentence (in this case, "people").

BUT THIS: <u>People</u> who do random acts of kindness for others experience many happy times.

2) Another way to correct a dangling modifier is to change the modifier to a dependent phrase.

Many happy times can be experienced *when people do random acts of kindness for others*.

By doing random acts of kindness for others, people can experience many happy times.

Exercise 1b. In these sentences add a word or phrase that the modifier can logically describe. In some cases, you may need to reword the sentence by, perhaps, adding a subject and/or verb. *Hint:* First, create a picture of each sentence in your mind. Then, correct the sentence so that your mental picture is logical.

1. With eighty miles still to drive, the highway was dark.

2. Flying over San Francisco, the Golden Gate Bridge looked awesome.

3. Coming to terms with her sexuality in light of her faith, the future looked brighter.

4. While in the wheelchair, you should stretch your legs so that blood continues to circulate.

5. Teaching is a high pressure field, but I still want to be one.

Arthur and Pulley

6. Using a dry sponge, the milk was wiped from the floor.

   _____

7. Rowing the boat across the lake, the cat became terrified.

   _____

8. Watching the sun rise, the weather grew hotter and hotter.

   _____

9. Engineering requires much mathematical ability; nevertheless, I want to be one.

   _____

10. Tired and sleepy, there were still three more hours to drive.

    _____

11. Having missed English class for seven days, my grade was in jeopardy.

    _____

12. To have a good marriage, trust is necessary.

    _____

13. Standing on the side of the road, the cars almost ran over us.

    _____

14. As an out-of-work, middle-aged man, it is difficult to get a date.

_____

15. On a bench in a park on a rainy night in 1996 was one of the greatest dates I ever had.

_____

16. Hate crimes and school shootings, Enrique thought he'd never see the day.

_____

17. Looking up at the stars, they fell down the riverbank.

_____

18. Growing up in the Deep South, the weather was always very humid.

_____

19. To pass your college classes, hard work and commitment are necessary qualities.

_____

20. As a person with high ambition and aspirations is difficult to find someone who understands the way it is.

_____

FAULTY PARALLELISM

Sentence parallelism enhances reading comprehension because it balances elements within a sentence. Parallelism exists when all corresponding elements in the sentence are equal, whether that means they are the same part of speech (nouns, adjectives, verbs, prepositions, etc.) or have the same grammatical structure.

1) Perhaps the easiest way to recognize whether or not parallelism exists is if the elements appear as items in a series as in the sentence below.

FAULTY: James went with Bobby *to the barber shop, to the football game, and then they went to the wrestling match.*

In this case, *to the barber shop* and *to the football game* are parallel, but *and then they went to the wrestling match* renders the series unparallel. The series demands that all the elements (in this case the prepositional phrases) be written equally. So, to correct the faulty parallelism, the sentence should be rewritten as:

PARALLEL: James went with Bobby *to the barber shop, to the football game,* and *to the wrestling match*.

FAULTY: Zacary often exercises by *swimming, jogging, and he also skates.*

PARALLEL: Zacary often exercises by *swimming, jogging,* and *skating.*

2) If two clauses are joined by a coordinating conjunction, parallelism will exist when both clauses have the same word order, as is illustrated in these sentences.

FAULTY: Brandon and Natika are two students **who** are never late for class and **that** always like to read the assignment.

PARALLEL: Brandon and Natika are two students **who** are never late for class and **who** always read the assignments.

3) Co-relative conjunctions (paired conjunctions) form another example of parallel structure:

PARALLEL: *Not only* does the choir sing every Sunday, *but* the choir *also* sings on Wednesday nights too.

Arthur and Pulley

Exercise 2a. Some of the sentences below are correct. Rewrite any of the following sentences that lack parallel structure:

1. To get to grandmother's house, Kari and I had to go over the river and through the woods.

   _____

2. In order to get an "A" in their classes, many students resort to crying, screaming, and then they start kicking.

   _____

3. Love and trust, faith and hope, devotion and commitment are all qualities that constitute a long-term friendship.

   _____

4. Alethea's boyfriend had tried everything he knew to win back her love—pleading, begging, and crying, and after that, buying gifts.

   _____

5. You can come with me to church and to school, or you can go with him to the party and to the club.

   _____

6. Mosquitoes are nasty little creatures that bite, sting, stab, and they suck your blood, too.

   _____

Arthur and Pulley   Page 53

7. I would love to live atop a mountain, swim in the ocean, dance among the stars and looking like soaring eagle.

   _____

8. Why do fools rage, evil men destroy, and sometimes why do the elite mock the simple?

   _____

9. I wonder as I wander.

   _____

10. When I finish doing my chores, I'm going to go shopping, go to the movies, pick up Gary, and settle into bed.

    _____.

MIXED CONSTRUCTIONS

A sentence with a mixed construction is yet another sentence fault that results in confusion and misinterpretation for the reader. A mixed sentence simply has two parts that are not compatible. They don't fit together; consequently, confusion in meaning results. Consider the following sentence:

After running for two hours was the reason he was exhausted.

To correct this type of mixed construction, you need to determine the focus of the sentence and revise it in such a way that it reflects the meaning you want to convey. Note the following revisions:

He was exhausted because he had run for two hours.

Because he had run for two hours, he was exhausted.

He was exhausted after he had run for two hours.

As another example, consider this mixed construction:

A compromise between Jeffrey and Margaret Ann would be the best relationship.

In the above sentence the subject, *compromise,* is equated with the complement, *relationship*, saying that a *compromise would be a relationship.* This is not a sensible statement: it makes no sense. The sentence can, however, be stated in such a way to make the writer's meaning more clear as in these revised sentences:

A compromise between Jeffrey and Margaret Ann would be the best way to ensure that they have a good relationship.

The way to the best relationship between Jeffrey and Margaret Ann would be a compromise between them.

Exercise 3a. If necessary, eliminate any unclear meaning due to mixed constructions in the following sentences:

1. By asking the teacher for advice about writing your paper is the best way to learn.

   _____

2. The old clothes that we found in the dark, dingy attic, we took to the church charity bazaar.

   _____

3. The students who had all of their assignments done, the teacher told them to stand next to their desks.

   _____

4. Because of too much late night dating and too many classes missed made Mario and Julio fail their exams.

   _____

Arthur and Pulley — Page 55

5. The beasts that had been tamed, their trainer took them to the circus owner.

    _____

6. After fighting with his parents for two hours was the reason he was so irritable.

    _____

7. Some kind of sacrifice by the citizens would be the best solution.

    _____

8. Practicing every day explains why she sings so well.

    _____

9. Although Mr. Robertson was found with the gun in his hand doesn't mean he should be charged with Mrs. Robertson's murder.

    _____

10. A bad cut is when you bleed for days.

    _____

WORD ORDER

Often, merely the way words are arranged in sentences determines whether or not your messages are clear. Early in your education, you learned that sentences contained nouns, verbs, and an object of the verb, usually in that order. It would be odd to see a "sentence" which read "Studies Matilda criminal justice." To eliminate confusion of ideas, sentences are put together in a certain order. In fact, because you are aware of correct sentence structure rules, you can re-arrange nonsensical sentences so that they make sense. Sometimes if the meaning you want to convey is unclear, you will have to rearrange the words for clarity. At other times, however, it is best to get rid of a word or two for the sake of clarity. Consider the following additional examples:

CONFUSING: It was during the day at the beginning when the chaos started.

CLEAR: *The chaos started at the beginning of the day.*

At the beginning of the day, the chaos started.

CONFUSING: Whenever Jamal would try to lift his legs, both of them, he would become agitated and fall almost.

CLEAR: *Whenever Jamal would try to lift both his legs, he would become agitated and almost fall.*

Jamal would become agitated and almost fall whenever he would try to lift both his legs.

Standard word order in sentences places the subject before the verb. This very clear and common pattern is effective, but occasionally the inverted word order, which places the verb before the subject, can create emphasis in your writing. Consider these sentences:

STANDARD: The manager walked *in;* the employee walked *out.*

INVERTED: *In* walked the manager; *out* walked the employee.

STANDARD: *The man* who gives to charitable causes *is fulfilled and happy.*

INVERTED: *Fulfilled and happy is the man* who gives to charitable causes.

Exercise 4a. If necessary, eliminate, add, or rearrange words or phrases in the following sentences to make the meaning clear:

1. In the middle of the night was when the Creeks ran with the moon.

Arthur and Pulley

2. There were holes, so many of them, in Juan's pocket to his suit that he lost all his money, nearly.

   _____

3. Can you believe it's 3 o'clock in afternoon already?

   _____

4. Manuel simply goes through his daily routine as if he has not a care in his whole life that he has to worry about.

   _____

5. Confused and bewildered when they walked into the room, Maurice said.

   _____

6. Demanding and imposing teachers always are, it seems.

   _____

7. Gary felt really and truly challenged when he was asked to move to London.

   _____

8. It was 1985 when all the chaos at Riverdale High School started.

   _____

9. I thought both Andreas and Enrique by now would have left the auditorium.

   _____

10. "You can make it if you try," my mother always said.

_____

Exercise 4b. Now change the *standard* word order to the *inverted* word order in the following sentences:

11. There are too few people visiting the museum today.

_____

12. After many disputes and arguments, there is finally a reconciliation made between Jamie and Jeremy.

_____

13. The cat comes in; the dog runs out.

_____

14. My daughter's primary confidant is her very wise boyfriend.

_____

15. From the upstairs bedroom came screeching sounds during the night.

_____

16. There were lots of people visiting me today.

_____

17. I couldn't care less if you get drunk and pass out.

_____

18. Marquetta got caught coming home late from the party.

___

19. I can never forgive Eric for the lie he told.

___

20. Friends are hard to come by these days.

___

Name_____ Date_____ Score_____

MASTERY TEST THREE

Now let's see what you've learned about misplaced and dangling modifiers, parallelism, mixed constructions, and word order. Correct any problems in the following sentences.

1. In many family homes, all the children sit down to dinner with their parents, especially in southeast Georgia.

2. Sliding and tumbling downhill, the parents just stood there watching the children.

3. Kim thought his friend, Ralph, would make him insane totally, but he ended up helping him.

4. I watched the boys and a few girls standing on a hill.

5. High school teachers earn more money than college professors generally.

6. Kimiko and Matsuo enjoy playing sports, riding bicycles, watching movies, and they like telling stories, too.

7. Mr. and Mrs. Schindler named their three daughters Faith, Hope, and they named one Charity.

8. Helio is usually, most of the time, on top of the world, or he is really, way, way down in the dumps.

9. Some people want to rekindle an old love affair so badly that they will do anything from swimming the deep blue sea to the purchase of diamonds and emeralds.

10. What's more important in your life: values and principles, silver and gold, or is it position and power?

11. With ten weeks of chemotherapy ahead, the future looked bleak.

12. A career in psychiatry involves a lot of drive and determination, but I still want to be one.

13. Even when sad and disappointed, you should still count your blessings.

14. Many joys can be found playing with your children in the park.

15. Running past the nurses' station in nothing but an open-backed gown, she fell into my waiting arms.

16. Since we had shopped for five hours was the reason we were so exhausted.

17. A compromise between the citizens of Edinburgh and the city government would be the best solution.

18. By obeying your parents and adhering to the Golden Rule is the best way to succeed.

19. By too much late night carousing is what made Greg and Saba fail their classes.

20. Changing jobs every other week is why she interviews so well.

21. It was while it was storming, in the middle of the night, when the lights went out and the dog ran away with the spoon.

22. When Charisse would try to lift her arms, both of them, to comb her hair, her tennis elbow got worse.

23. In the early morning hours was when Mel wanted to see Linda.

24. Dazed and confused when they heard the news of his accident, Shelby said.

25. Looking sad, lonely, and forlorn, they stood at the head of the casket.

CHAPTER FIVE: DICTION AND STYLE

Diction and style in writing have to do with word choices and how those words are arranged in sentences to make ideas clear. The objective is to choose words, sentence structure, and paragraph arrangements to convey your message as strongly and effectively as possible. Consequently, there is no room left on the part of the reader for misinterpretation or misunderstanding of your ideas. Words should, therefore, be chosen carefully, and your writing should be cohesive, vivid, and specific to bring life to it. Compare these two excerpts about a student's best friend:

A. *My friend is a wonderful person. She does a lot of things for me, and I can always count on her when I need a helping hand. Getting into some rough situations, I have always had her to see me through hard times. Where I would be without her, I can't imagine.*

While the language and message above does have some degree of clarity, the ideas and their impact would be greatly enhanced if some of the words and phrases were changed or rearranged and specifics were used:

B. *My friend, Monetha, is a wonderful person. She does so much for me. When I am having trouble passing a class because I don't understand the professor's lectures or the homework assignments, Monetha is always available to tutor me. She comes to my house, or we meet at the library and stay there for hours studying together. Then, she even takes me to Hardee's or Shoney's to eat before she helps me clean my apartment. It's amazing how I can always count on Monetha when I need a shoulder to lean on. You see, I get into some rough situations sometimes, but she invariably sees me through them. Last month, I lost my grandmother in a car accident. I was both angry and depressed over her death. As usual, Monetha was there to console me and to make it all better with kind words and affection. An event I will never forget occurred last year when I had to confront my parents about a boy I was seeing, and Monetha backed me up. Again, she saved my life! I don't know where I would be without her.*

In this paragraph the reader has a better grasp of the kind of friend Monetha is and how she helped the student. The reader also gets a glimpse into the personalities of both the student and Monetha. Thus, the reader gains better comprehension because the writer gave specifics, was vivid in the descriptions, wrote well-structured sentences, and presented the reader with a cohesive piece of writing.

APPROPRIATE WORD CHOICE

The process of choosing the right word is not always easy. In fact, it can become complex, especially since no clear rule applies for distinguishing the right word from the wrong one. The same word may be appropriate in one case and inappropriate in another. Different audiences and different occasions call for varying levels of words. It is essential that, as a writer, you consider the level of formality needed, the range of words you have to choose from, and the connotations of each word you are considering. For instance, you might think it strange if your history teacher said that Martin Luther King, Jr. was the *dude* who was shot and killed in the name of equal rights, although the terms *man, guy, male, and dude* essentially mean the same thing. In the same vein, you would probably not say to your parents, *"I need some bread and a ride so I can take out this real babe, tonight."* Instead, you would more likely say, *"I need some money and the car so I can go on a date with a really intelligent girl, tonight."* You need to determine whether words need to be <u>formal</u>, as in research papers, formal reports, and some essays, or <u>informal</u>, as in conversational writing which calls for slang or colloquialisms. Consider the sample alternative words and phrases that follow:

FORMAL	INFORMAL OR SLANG
affluent, wealthy	in the dough, has lots of cash/bread
impoverished	poor, in the poorhouse, flat broke
inebriated	drunk, wasted, plastered
relaxing	chillin
money	bread, dough
vehicle	car, ride, wheels
nervous/tense	high strung, bugged out
television	TV, the tube
man of leisure	couch potato
seductive	sexy, fine
incorrect, wrong	whacked

Arthur and Pulley   Page 65

Exercise 1a. Give the informal phrase/slang for the words or phrases below.

1. Police
2. Money
3. Automobile
4. Man
5. Woman
6. Exhausted
7. Famished
8. Killed
9. Weak person
10. Great

Even though there are no absolute rules that distinguish standard (formal) and non-standard (informal) usage, when speaking or writing always avoid using terms such as *theirselves, hisself, anywheres, nohow,* and *ain't.*

Exercise 1b. Write five currently used slang experssions and give their formal counterparts.

1. _____
2. _____
3. _____
4. _____
5. _____

CONNOTATIVE LANGUAGE

Similar to informal word choice is the use of *connotative* language. The connotative meaning of a word is not explicit or immediately apparent as is its denotative (dictionary) definition. Instead, connotation refers to ideas implied but not directly indicated by a word. It suggests what the word means to you emotionally and/or socially, beyond the dictionary's meaning. For example, the word *home* generally evokes more emotion than is suggested by its dictionary definition of "a dwelling place" or even its synonym *house*. *Home* usually suggests connotations of warmth, pleasantness, love, and security. On the other hand, for some students *home* could have negative connotations as well, depending on what their particular experiences were. In addition, *home* could also refer to institutions for sick, elderly, or mentally ill persons.

Words used *connotatively* oftentimes express the feeling and emotion of the writer. For instance, because many *odors* are unpleasant and the word *odor* connotes something undesirable, in most cases, you would most likely not say, "I love the *odor* of freshly baked glazed ham." Rather, you would say something that sounds more positive, such as "I love the *aroma* of freshly baked glazed ham." Conversely, you would probably not hear the statement, "The *aroma* of the garbage at the dump is putrifying!"

Exercise 2a. In the following sentences, choose the formal or informal word based on the context of each statement:

1. The American Ambassador claimed that his (*suitcase* or *stuff*) was lost due to the negligence of airport security personnel.

2. Let my (*suitcase* or *bags*) go before I really get mad!

3. The invention of the (*phone* or *telephone*) so many years ago has proven to be an absolutely ingenious move on the part of Alexander Graham Bell.

4. Could you grab the (phone or telephone); it's ringing off the hook!

5. Please (*fill out* or *execute*) the documents at your earliest convenience and return them to our attorneys.

6. Just (*fill out* or *execute*) the papers and give them to one of the bosses.

Exercise 2b. Now, indicate which of the following sentences make use of formal and informal word choices:

7. ____ I really hate his guts!

8. ____ I really abhor that corporate executive officer!

9. ____ In ninth grade, I would always get so sick during lunch, and one day I threw up all over my teacher.

10. ____ The doctor diagnosed that the regurgitating was due to toxins ingested by the patient.

Exercise 2c. Write the connotation of the italicized expression in the following sentences.

1. Lolita has been depressed for a while now, but I know that deep down she's a real *trooper*!

2. My cousin has been depressed for a while now, and I'm afraid that she'll *take herself out*.

3. Tears *flood* my eyes every time I remember him.

4. Take your *mitts* off my book bag!

5. Mr. Martinez is a real *klutz*.

COMMONLY CONFUSED WORDS

Master the correct use of these most commonly confused words by learning what each word means:

1. it's / its

It's is a contraction meaning *it is,* as in

It's a beautiful day! or *It is a beautiful day!*

Its is the possessive form of *it; its* shows ownership, as in

The pet comes quickly when its master calls.

2. lie / lay / laid

Lie is the present tense verb form when referencing human beings, as in

> *I need to lie down and rest this tired and weary body.*

Lie is also a noun and verb meaning to speak an untruth, as in

> *You didn't really have to tell me that lie!* Or

> *Why did you lie to Jennifer?*

Lay is the past tense of the verb form of *lie,* when referencing human beings, as in

> *I lay down for two hours; then, I went out.*

Laid is the past tense and past participle of the verb form of *lie* when referencing objects, as in

> *He laid the book on the table.*

3. then / than

Then indicates time, transition, or that some action is to follow, as in

> *It was then time to go home.* or

> *First, Alberta went to church; then, she went home.*

Than suggests that a comparison or choice is being made, as in

> *The night before an exam, Jeff would rather go out drinking than stay home and study.* Or

> *Rather than go to sleep and have pleasant dreams, let's just act them out!*

4. there / their / they're

There refers to time, distance, space, or location, as in

> *Why doesn't he move over there and leave me alone?* or

> *Is there a place we can go and have some privacy?*

Their indicates possession or ownership, as in

>*I really don't care; what Jim and Susie do in private is their business.* Or

>*All of their friends are my enemies.*

They're is a contraction meaning *they are,* as in

>*They're all bad neighbors!* Or

>*Whenever I need friends to count on, they are always there.*

5. to / too / two

To refers to place, as in

>*May I go with you to the market?*

Too means also, in addition to, in excess of, similarly, likewise, as in

>*I, too, would like to date Johnathon and Brian.* Or

>*Can they both be dumb and dangerous, too?*

Two means the numerical 2, as in

>*I'm so tired that I could sleep for two days.*

Exercise 3a. Make corrections, if necessary, to the following sentences which may contain commonly confused words:

1. Carlos has been waiting for *two* days *to* return *to* his homeland, but he is still *too* afraid to board an airplane.

2. *They're* going to be late for the party, but they'll have fun once they get *there* and get *their* groove on.

3. I find it so amazing that Amanda and Coretta would rather go to Barbados *than* the Virgin Islands and *then* stop over in Florida on *their* way home.

Arthur and Pulley   Page 70

4. Artemus swore that he would not *lie* the book down until he finished reading it.

5. *Its* a lovely spring day; I hope *its* not going to rain, later, and spoil *it's* splendor.

Now, create sentences of your own that illustrate the appropriate use of commonly confused words:

6. _____

7. _____

8. _____

9. _____

10. _____

TRANSITIONS

Transitional words and phrases serve to move your sentences and paragraphs along smoothly and with a natural flow without awkward interruptions. Transitions prepare the reader for what is to follow. Furthermore, they aid coherence by showing the relationships among sentences. By making logical and sequential connections, transitional words and phrases tie together the ideas in paragraphs.

Read the following paragraph which lacks transitional words and phrases:

Clara Bell certainly made a change for the better by leaving the big city of Boston. She went back to Statesboro, Georgia and finished college. She found a husband and a peaceful, quiet neighborhood in which to live. She had two adorable children, a boy and a girl. They grew into fine, wholesome individuals who excelled in school. Clara worked as an interior designer where she gained the respect and admiration of her peers. She was diagnosed with terminal cancer and refused to give up hope for her life. She beat the odds and is living and thriving.

The above paragraph does have a clear unifying idea, but the exact chronological relationships among events is not clear. This is because there are no transitional expressions used, making the paragraph sound like just a list of unconnected events.

Now, read the next paragraph which uses transitional words and phrases that provide the links to clarify the chronological order of events in the paragraph.

Clara Bell certainly made a change for the better by leaving the big city of Boston. After a one year stint there, she moved back to Statesboro, Georgia. A few months later, she enrolled at the university. Consequently, she earned a degree in interior design. While working, she met her future husband. After marrying, they found a peaceful, quiet neighborhood in which to live. Within two years, she had two adorable children, a boy and a girl. During their childhoods and adolescence, they grew into fine, wholesome individuals who excelled in school. In the meantime, Clara worked in an architectural firm where she gained the respect and admiration of her peers. Later on, however, at the peak of her career, she was diagnosed with terminal cancer. Still, she worked, refusing to give up hope for her life. Finally, after a long battle that lasted several years, she beat the odds and is yet living and thriving.

Note the following list of commonly used transitions:

again	also	too	next	last
next	besides	finally	furthermore	still
moreover	so	afterward	now	as soon as
meanwhile	until	later	eventually	after
before	earlier	soon	during	for instance
immediately	similarly	now	likewise	yet
but	instead	subsequently	however	even
nonetheless	then	nevertheless	although	granted
example	for	consequently	therefore	so
in contrast	in addition			

Exercise 4a. Now, fill in the blanks of the paragraph below with transitional words/phrases from this list. If you find a word/phrase from the list on page 71, and it is appropriate, feel free to use it.

subsequently	nonetheless	during	furthermore
consequently	in addition	immediately	although

Arthur and Pulley   Page 72

Discrimination in white churches and the need for a separate spiritual community life led to the establishment of Black churches in the South. _____ not as massively organized or centralized as the Methodists in the North, Baptists gained some followers in the South. The Baptists had congregational independence which helped free Blacks establish their own churches unhampered by church polity and structure. _____ the first African Baptist churches emerged in the late 1770s in South Carolina, Virginia and Georgia led by Black ministers as Georgia Liele and Andrew Bryan.

The Methodists predominated in the upper South's cities. In one Norfolk Methodist church sat men on the left and women on the right. _____ the free Blacks were seated apart from the slaves. These class divisions appeared more frequently in the cities of the Lower South where light-skinned elites purchased pews in the white churches rather than worship in their own. _____ along the Gulf, free Black Protestants often worshiped with the Catholic free persons of color to gain the advantages of certificates of marriage and baptism needed to prove freedom.

Southern whites feared the power of the Black church. _____ white mobs attacked such churches and legislators created laws to restrict its power. _____ the 1820s, white supervision was required to form these churches. Following Nat Turner's rebellion, whites shut Black churches, barred Black preachers, required the presence of white ministers, and shut down Black schools. _____ Richmond free Blacks sought permission to establish a separate Black meeting house. Ignored, they took their petition to the local Baptist church. With no support, they _____ met in homes and alleys to organize and worship. The Black church movement could not be stopped.

-Salem, pp. 136-137

Exercise 4b. On a separate piece of paper, rewrite the following paragraph, inserting transitional words and phrases so that the chronological order of events is clear:

It has been awfully difficult for Justin to adjust to his newfound freedom. He never contacts any old friends back home. He started making new friends over the Internet and staying out half the night on weekends. His apartment is in a mess. His appearance is shabby. His personality is very rude and arrogant. Justin argues and fights all the time. He has begun to drink and even use drugs on a regular basis. He wrecked his car in a road rage encounter and was almost killed. He's in the hospital, tied to tubes and machines. The doctors don't hold out much hope for his recovery. My goodness, how tragic Justin's life has become.

WORDINESS

Wordiness occurs when a number of unnecessary words are used: they are often repetitious terms; they do not help clarify your statements, and usually leave your sentences unclear. You want your writing to be concise (direct and to the point). Wordy writing is not so. Wordiness actually irritates readers because it demands that they mentally "get rid of excess and unnecessary words" so that sentences can relay their messages. Concise writing uses words economically; consequently, it avoids abstract and convoluted sentence structures.

DON'T WRITE:	It is obvious that we missed the bus.
DO WRITE:	Obviously, we missed the bus.
DON'T WRITE:	There was, in fact, a girl named Marsha Brown who won the award.
DO WRITE:	Marsha Brown won the award.
DON'T WRITE:	The Atlanta Braves were defeated by a score of 22 to 7 by the Los Angeles Dodgers in a baseball game last Monday night.
DO WRITE:	Last Monday, The Atlanta Braves were defeated 22 to 7 by the Los Angeles Dodgers.

Exercise 5a. Look at the following constructions. Rewrite the sentences, eliminating any wordiness that interferes with clarity and meaning:

1. The absolute final total amount of pennies collected was $800.23.

_____

2. It is a proven fact that boys have just as difficult a life as girls have a difficult life.

_____

3. Marcella really and truly wants to date Raphael, but Raphael keeps refusing all of Marcella's not so subtle advances.

_____

4. *The Notebook* is a short novel which was on the *New York Times* bestseller list of short novels for a little longer than one year.

_____

5. If you stomp on my feet and toes, I will cry out loud because of the resulting hurt and pain.

_____

IDIOMATIC USAGE

Idioms are generally set language expressions that have interpretations contrary to the their literal meanings. These expressions are often characteristic of particular geographic regions. Idiomatic language does not follow any rules; it has become fixed through tradition. Consider this example:

      A. Jeffrey comes in every day with a *chip on his shoulder*.

(Certainly, Jeffrey doesn't literally have a *chip* on his *shoulder*; rather, he comes in with a bad attitude or disposition.)

      B. It's raining *cats and dogs*.

(Cats and dogs can't literally be falling from the sky; rather, this expression suggests the force with which the rain comes down.)

      C. My boyfriend makes me feel like I'm *walking on air*.

(No one can actually walk on air, but my boyfriend makes me feel very happy and carefree.)

Exercise 6a. Now, see if you can interpret the following idiomatic expressions:

1. Mariah *dances her feet off* as she sings.

   _____

2. Sean often says that he wants to *move up* in the world.

   _____

3. Many frustrated people just need to *get a grip*.

   _____

4. Linda and Hubert were clammy and sweaty because it was *hot as Hades*.

   _____

5. You need to stop wearing your *heart on your sleeve* .

   _____

Name_____Date_____Score_____

MASTERY TEST FOUR

Now let's see what you've learned about correct word choice/confused words, transitions, wordiness, and idioms by rewriting the following sentences where necessary, eliminating any problem with diction or style:

1. Sometimes my algebra teacher acts as if he has gone loco.

_____

2. I'm going to lose my boyfriend if I don't buy me some wheels soon.

_____

3. Yesterday, Raphael ate a bunch of candy and got sick.

_____

4. Its so dark outside that I can't see my hand before my face.

_____

5. Because Jonathan was so tired after his wrestling match, he laid down to rest for an hour.

_____

6. I would rather keep my mouth shut and be thought a fool rather then open it and remove all doubt.

_____

7. They're wounds from the car accident will take months to heal.

_____

8. Likewise, James and John flew from Japan to Mexico.

_____

9. After going all the way to Hawaii from Tokyo, Mr. and Mrs. Valentino eventually left for Australia.

_____

10. It is ironic that Bill failed his math quiz after studying so hard.

_____

11. As a matter of fact, a man named Marshall Thompson was honored at the meeting that was held on Tuesday night.

_____

| Arthur and Pulley | Page 79 |

12. Can't we all just get along and be friends together?

_____

13. Maurice vowed not to go to any more parties, even though he thinks their a lot of fun.

_____

14. Darvin wanted to attend the University of Arizona; nevertheless, he ended up enrolling at Morristown College.

_____

15. It's storming like mad.

_____

16. Jeffrey complained that he was hungry as a horse.

_____

17. The heat outside is really sweltering today.

_____

18. If you slap my face, I will cry very loudly because of the pain and sting that will result because of the blow.

_____

19. Can't you just see me now with all of those scholars and graduates getting their degrees and diplomas during the graduation ceremony?
_____

20. He is such a phony human being.
_____

21. Tristan and Kristin went on there merry way after they had visited the cemetery.
_____

22. Nick really can't get into that music.
_____

23. Jessica really, really, really thinks highly of Chinese and Mexican foods.
_____

24. Could you lay down and rest with little Susie for a while?
_____

25. Why can't we two be just friends instead of being friends and lovers?
_____

PRACTICE EXIT EXAMS

GENERAL DIRECTIONS FOR PRACTICE EXIT EXAMS

IN THE PASSAGES THAT FOLLOW, CERTAIN WORDS AND PHRASES ARE UNDERLINED AND NUMBERED. IN THE RIGHT-HAND COLUMN, YOU WILL FIND ALTERNATIVES FOR EACH UNDERLINED PART. YOU ARE TO CHOOSE THE ALTERNATIVE THAT BEST

1) EXPRESSES THE IDEA
2) MAKES THE STATEMENT APPROPRIATE FOR STANDARD WRITTEN ENGLISH
3) IS WORDED MOST CONSISTENTLY WITH THE STYLE AND TONE OF THE PASSAGE AS A WHOLE

IF YOU THINK THE ORIGINAL VERSION IS BEST, CHOOSE "NO CHANGE." FOR EACH QUESTION IN THE TEST, CHOOSE THE ALTERNATIVE YOU CONSIDER BEST AND BLACKEN THE CORRESPONDING SPACE ON YOUR SCANTRON PROVIDED IN THIS TEXT. SOME QUESTIONS MAY REQUIRE YOU TO READ SEVERAL SENTENCES BEFORE OR AFTER THE PHRASE IN ORDER TO CHOOSE THE BEST ANSWER.

Name_____Date_____Score_____

PRACTICE EXIT EXAM ONE

In the late nineteenth century, (1) <u>professional baseball players</u> and most other professional team sports (2) <u>prohibited</u> interracial competition. White players played (3) <u>for the highest salaries, in the best stadiums, before</u> the most spectators.

But on April 18, 1946, the sports world (4) <u>had been focused</u> on a baseball field in Jersey (5) <u>City; It</u> was the opening day for the Jersey City Giants of the International League. (6) <u>There</u> opponents were the Montreal Royals, the Brooklyn Dodgers' leading farm team.

GO ON TO THE NEXT PAGE

1. A. NO CHANGE
   B. professional baseball
   C. the professions of baseball that is professional
   D. the professional baseball game

2. A. NO CHANGE
   B. prohibiting
   C. have prohibited
   D. did prohibit

3. A. NO CHANGE
   B. for the highest salaries, in the best stadiums, and before
   C. for the highest salaries, in the best stadiums before
   D. for the highest salaries in the best stadiums before

4. A. NO CHANGE
   B. was focused
   C. was focusing
   D. focused

5. A. NO CHANGE
   B. city, it
   C. city. It
   D. city: it

6. A. NO CHANGE
   B. There
   C. Their
   D. They're

(7) Playing second base for the Royals. Was Jackie Roosevelt Robinson, a pigeon-toed, highly competitive, (8) and he was a marvelously talented African-American athlete. The stadium was filled with curious and excited spectators, and in the press box sports writers from New York, Philadelphia, Baltimore, and cities further west fidgeted with their typewriters. It was not just another season-opening game. Professional baseball, (9) Americas national game, was about to be integrated. In the third inning, Robinson took his second turn at bat. With runners on first and second, he lashed out at the first pitch and hit it over the left field fence 300 feet away. In the field, he was tough, intense, and smart, a reverse image of the stereotypical black athlete. It (10) became a fine day for Robinson and his supporters.

-Martin, pp. 948-949

7. A. NO CHANGE
B. Playing second base for the Royals, was Jackie
C. Playing second base for the Royals; was Jackie
D. Playing second base for the Royals

8. A. NO CHANGE
B. marvelously talented
C. also marvelously talented
D. and he was also a marvelously talented

9. A. NO CHANGE
B. American
C. Americas'
D. America's

10. A. NO CHANGE
B. was
C. was becoming
D. had become

Mental illness can play a role in a criminal case in two (11) ways. First, it must be asked whether the (12) prosecutor is sane enough to be placed on trial. Second, it must be established whether the defendant was sane at the time of the act. Defendants must be mentally competent to stand trial so as to understand the legal proceedings against (13) them. The legal standard for determining competency to stand trial was established back in (14) 1960–it was at that time when the U.S. Supreme Court held that a person is incompetent to stand trial if (15) they 1) lacks the ability to consult with a lawyer with a reasonable degree of understanding and 2) lacks a rational and factual understanding of the legal proceedings.

A defendant who (16) was found incompetent to stand trial (17) would not go free but rather can be committed to a

11. A. NO CHANGE
    B. ways, first,
    C. ways; first,
    D. ways first

12. A. NO CHANGE
    B. defendant
    C. judge
    D. jury

13. A. NO CHANGE
    B. theirs
    C. the defendants
    D. the police

14. A. NO CHANGE
    B. 1960...It
    C. 1960, it
    D. 1960. It

15. A. NO CHANGE
    B. it
    C. he or she
    D. the incompetent

16. A. NO CHANGE
    B. would be
    C. is
    D. wants to be

17. A. NO CHANGE
    B. will
    C. could
    D. does

mental institution and can be tried after recovering competency. Courts have (18) held up that a person may be detained in a mental institution for "a reasonable period" (19) for achievement of competency to stand trial. Some courts have interpreted this (20) period, to be no more than the maximum sentence that would be imposed for the crime if the person were convicted of it.

-Albanese, p. 157

18. A. NO CHANGE
    B. held
    C. held it up
    D. held on to it

19. A. NO CHANGE
    B. competing for achievement
    C. to achieve competency
    D. for achieving of competency

20. A. NO CHANGE
    B. period – to
    C. period; to
    D. period to

Arthur and Pulley

Having a pet in the family can make you (21) be feeling like a kid again. You get to run around, throw balls, get chased and just plain (22) acts ridiculous. And since most pets love taking a good romp–vets recommend getting out for at least 20 minutes twice a day–you both get some vigorous exercise in the bargain.

This is true not only for (23) dogs but in some cases for cats as well. In fact, walking a cat has some advantages over strolling with a canine counterpart. Cats don't lift their legs at every stop, constantly sniff the ground, or (24) then they tug on the leash. Cats love getting out of the house and going for walks, particularly if you get (25) cats used to it when they're young.

Cats wriggle out of collars (26) easily; so many vets recommend using a

21. A. NO CHANGE
    B. feels
    C. feeling
    D. feel

22. A. NO CHANGE
    B. act
    C. acting
    D. act up

23. A. NO CHANGE
    B. dogs, but
    C. dogs; but
    D. dogs–but

24. A. NO CHANGE
    B. tug on the leash
    C. consequently, tugging on the leash
    D. lastly tugged on the leash

25. A. NO CHANGE
    B. these cats
    C. the cats
    D. them

26. A. NO CHANGE
    B. easily, so
    C. easily–so
    D. easily so

Arthur and Pulley

harness instead of the usual choke collar. To get (27) her used to the idea, first put on the harness without the leash. Once she's used to the harness, snap on the leash and (28) taken some practice walks around the house. When you both feel (29) comfortable. Head outdoors for an enjoyable jaunt; but don't expect your cat to heel like a dog. (30) Basically; she's going to be walking you!

-Hoffman, p. 13

27. A. NO CHANGE
    B. your cat
    C. him
    D. yourself

28. A. NO CHANGE
    B. taking
    C. take
    D. took

29. A. NO CHANGE
    B. comfortable–head
    C. comfortable; head
    D. comfortable, head

30. A. NO CHANGE
    B. Basically,
    C. Basically...she's
    D. Basically she's

He (31) <u>meet</u> her gaze and stared down pointedly at the Red Rose embroidered on his coat. How strange, she thought.

"His Grace (32) <u>want</u> you to come to him, my lady," said Raulin.

"Why does he send for me in secret?" She pressed her hands tight against (33) <u>Katherine's</u> breast to still the jumping of her heart, but she stood very quiet, leaning against the table.

"Because (34) <u>sense</u> his wife's funeral he has seen nobody but me, nor does he wish to, my lady, except now—you."

Katherine and Raulin (35) <u>riden</u> back to the Savoy in silence. He led her to a small wooden door which he unlocked. Katherine swallowed, and (36) <u>mounted the steps</u>. They ended on the next floor where there was another door,

31. A. NO CHANGE
    B. was meeting
    C. meets
    D. met

32. A. NO CHANGE
    B. have wanted
    C. wanting
    D. wants

33. A. NO CHANGE
    B. she
    C. her
    D. the lady's

34. A. NO CHANGE
    B. since
    C. cents
    D. sence

35. A. NO CHANGE
    B. ride
    C. rode
    D. had ridden

36. A. NO CHANGE
    B. the steps mounted
    C. the steps she mounted
    D. steps mounted

Arthur and Pulley

concealed by a painted tapestry. Raulin pushed it aside and knocked on the carved oak door. A voice said, "Enter!" Raulin held the (37) <u>door then</u> shut it after Katherine, and went away.

    Katherine walked in quietly, her head lifted high, her cloak clutched around her. The Duke was sitting on a (38) <u>goldish-golden, gold-cushioned</u>, window seat gazing out over the river. She knelt and taking his hand, kissed it in homage. While she (39) <u>knelt. Her</u> cloak loosened and her hood fell back. He touched her curling rain-dampened hair.

    "It is the color of carnelians," he (40) <u>said "the</u> gem that heals anger. If only it could heal sorrow. . ." He spoke as though to himself, in a low, faltering voice.

    -Seton, pp. 201-202

37. A. NO CHANGE
    B. door, then
    C. door; then
    D. door–then

38. A. NO CHANGE
    B. golden-goldish cushioned
    C. gold-cushioned
    D. goldy-gold cushioned

39. A. NO CHANGE
    B. knelt, her
    C. knelt; her
    D. knelt her

40. A. NO CHANGE
    B. said. "the
    C. said. the
    D. said, "the

PRACTICE EXIT EXAM TWO

In life girls(1), it is said, have it much worse than boys, but in-depth research shows that girls and boys each have their own (2) painful equal sufferings. To say girls have it worse than (3) boys, is to put on blinders. Consider these facts: parents talk to, (4) and then they cuddle, and breast-feed their boy infants significantly less than their girl infants. Male infants also suffer a 25 percent higher mortality than female infants; boys are twice as likely as girls to suffer from autism and more likely to suffer birth defects. The majority of (5) schizophrenics – are boys. The majority of retarded children are boys; emotionally disturbed boys outnumber (6) girl's 4 to 1. Learning disabled boys outnumber girls 2 to 1, and boys are twice as likely as

1. A. NO CHANGE
   B. it is said
   C. ; it is said
   D. , it is said;

2. A. NO CHANGE
   B. equally painful sufferings
   C. equally painfully sufferings
   D. sufferings that are equally in pain

3. A. NO CHANGE
   B. boys; is
   C. boys -- is
   D. boys is

4. A. NO CHANGE
   B. cuddling
   C. cuddle
   D. to cuddle

5. A. NO CHANGE
   B. schizophrenics are
   C. schizophrenics, are
   D. schizophrenics; are

6. A. NO CHANGE
   B. girls'
   C. girls
   D. girl is

girls to be the victims of physical abuse.

(7) <u>Lastly</u> boys are four times as likely as girls to commit suicide. As kids get older, (8) <u>they</u> seem to have more opportunity and more encouragement than boys to get advanced education. In recent years, females out matriculated males in both college and graduate school.

For the last few (9) <u>decades. Our</u> cultural microscope has focused on the oppression of girls and women. That focus has led us to many gains in public consciousness, national policy, and private life. Now the lens must focus on boys too. For every boy who feels powerful at home or in his neighborhood there is another boy who (10) <u>felt</u> lost. For every football star there are far more male drug addicts, teenage alcoholics, high school dropouts, and juvenile delinquents. Boys are in pain.

-Gurian, pp. xvii-xviii

7. A. NO CHANGE
B. Lastly, boys
C. Lastly; boys
D. Lastly . . . boys

8. A. NO CHANGE
B. them
C. girls
D. boys

9. A. NO CHANGE
B. decades our
C. decades; our
D. decades -- our

10. A. NO CHANGE
B. is feeling
C. feels
D. has felt

Arthur and Pulley

Edward II was clearly a Plantagenet. He was as tall, strong, golden-haired and good-looking as his (11) father. But inside this magnificent shell there was no king. He made no effort to rule his subjects. He (12) cares nothing for the duties of a king. His only desire was to use the advantages of (13) Edward's position to enrich his friends and amuse himself. In London he was joined by the best of his friends, Piers Gaveston, a handsome knight with an eye to fame. (14) She had been Edward's close companion since childhood. Edward's demonstrations of affection toward Piers were extravagant. In spite of his preference for (15) Piers. Edward II married Isabella of France. Many of the wedding presents, though, (16) was given away to the favorite, and at his coronation he shocked the Court by

11. A. NO CHANGE
    B. father, but
    C. father. but
    D. father; but

12. A. NO CHANGE
    B. has cared
    C. cared
    D. hadn't cared

13. A. NO CHANGE
    B. his father's
    C. his
    D. him

14. A. NO CHANGE
    B. He
    C. Hisself
    D. They

15. A. NO CHANGE
    B. Piers, Edward
    C. Piers Edward
    D. Piers. . .Edward

16. A. NO CHANGE
    B. were gave
    C. given
    D. were given

demonstrating that he preferred the couch of Piers to that of the Queen. (17) Gaveston himself did nothing to quell the hatred and jealousy that the King's generosity aroused in the hearts of the nobles; he was playing a dangerous game. Though exiled many times, Piers appeared openly at the Christmas Court (18) during the holiday season and the yuletide a year after Edward's coronation. Enraged, his enemies hunted him down and murdered him.

Isabella (19) too, had her revenge. Sent to France as a peacemaker in 1325, she joined Roger Mortimer who had barely escaped from the Tower of London a few years before. Together they returned to England, and Edward was deposed and sent to the dungeon of Berkeley Castle. There his jailers,

17. A. NO CHANGE
B. Himself Gaveston did nothing
C. Nothing himself did Gaveston do
D. Gaveston doing nothing himself

18. A. NO CHANGE
B. in the yuletide, holiday season
C. Omit underlined portion
D. during the holiday season and during the yuletide

19. A. NO CHANGE
B. , too;
C. , too—
D. , too,

having failed to starve him to death, satisfied their order to leave no mark on his body. They made sure his injuries were (20) internal, and Edward II died a horrible death.

-Fraser, pp. 88-91;96

20. A. NO CHANGE
    B. internal. And
    C. Internal, and
    D. internal; and,

Arthur and Pulley

Rural (21) Americans especially those in the South, have long been misunderstood by other segments of the population. Some folks think that (22) a fellow just because he has a gun rack in the back window of his pickup that he's on his way to shoot a bunch of Democrats. (23) Democrats also think that grits grow on trees. And possibly their biggest misconception of all is that the (24) pink plastic flamingos positioned in many front yards are "tacky."

Nothing could be further from the truth. Tasteful, well-bred southerners normally paint the trunks of the trees in their yards white, (25) lining their driveways with old tires (also painted white), plant flowers between the tires, and place at least three pink flamingos strategically about the lawn. Common

21. A. NO CHANGE
    B. Americans, especially
    C. Americans; especially
    D. Americans—especially

22. A. NO CHANGE
    B. just because a fellow has
    C. because just a fellow has
    D. just because of a fellow's

23. A. NO CHANGE
    B. Folks
    C. Americans
    D. He

24. A. NO CHANGE
    B. pink and plastic flamingos
    C. flamingos that are pink and plastic
    D. plastic pinkish flamingos

25. A. NO CHANGE
    B. line
    C. having lined
    D. lined

riffraff, (26) consequently, decorate their yards by taking the tires off of a '52 Studebaker and putting the automobile on cement blocks beside the house.

My boyhood friend, Weyman C. (27) Wannamaker. Had a dozen plastic pink flamingos in his yard. Weyman's mother was president of the local garden (28) club; and her yard was the annual winner of the house beautiful award in our community. Mrs. Wannamaker, (29) having been a woman of exceeding taste and breeding, complemented her flamingos with a ceramic hen being followed by her baby chicks, and various other lawn statuary including ducks and deer and one marvelous piece in the form of a fat sumo wrestler, which she got for free.

Mrs. Wannamaker's yard was also quite impressive at Christmas.

26. A. NO CHANGE
    B. henceforth
    C. next
    D. meanwhile

27. A. NO CHANGE
    B. Wannamaker; had
    C. Wannamaker, had
    D. Wannamaker had

28. A. NO CHANGE
    B. club: and
    C. club—and
    D. club, and

29. A. NO CHANGE
    B. being
    C. was
    D. is

(30) <u>Their</u> annual decoration included Santa's sleigh being pulled by—you guessed it—eight pink flamingos.

-Grizzard, pp. 161-163

30. A. NO CHANGE
B. It's
C. Her
D. His

In the (31) world of classical ancient Greece and Rome, the making of art was generally viewed as a manual profession. Art was taught in (32) workshops. Greek vase painting illustrates this workshop tradition. Apprentice vase painters, some of them (33) female. Worked side-by-side with the master of the shop. Women must have been given the lesser positions within the workshop, for no Greek vases signed by (34) the master are known.

The Middle Ages continued to identify art as a manual profession. Artists formed (35) guilds: legal organizations rather like trade unions. These guilds (36) not only assured professional standards but also reinforced the distinction between the mechanical arts and the so-called liberal arts. During the Middle Ages, liberal arts

31. A. NO CHANGE
    B. ancient Greece and Rome's classical world
    C. Greece's and Rome's classical world of the ancients
    D. classical world of ancient Greece and Rome

32. A. NO CHANGE
    B. workshops, Greek
    C. workshops: Greek
    D. workshops . . . Greek

33. A. NO CHANGE
    B. female, worked
    C. female; worked
    D. female worked

34. A. NO CHANGE
    B. a woman
    C. women
    D. masters

35. A. NO CHANGE
    B. guilds; legal
    C. guilds. . .legal
    D. guilds legal

36. A. NO CHANGE
    B. omit "but"
    C. omit "not"
    D. omit "not only"

(37) encompassed arithmetic geometry astronomy music theory, grammar, and logic.

This traditional classification of the visual arts as mechanical (38) is transformed during the Renaissance. Both artists and writers began to emphasize the scientific and intellectual aspects of (39) art; it was argued, for example, that arithmetic was needed by the artist for the study of proportion, and that geometry figured in the proper calculation of perspective. The artist was beginning to be seen as an educated professional versed in both the practice and (40) art's theory. The new attitude that the artist was a skilled and educated individual was accompanied by a new social status. Artists became the companions of intellectuals, princes, and emperors.

-Wilkins, et. al., p, 31

37. A. NO CHANGE
B. encompassed: arithmetic, geometry astronomy
C. encompassed arithmetic, geometry, astronomy,
D. encompassed; arithmetic, geometry, astronomy

38. A. NO CHANGE
B. being
C. having been
D. was

39. A. NO CHANGE
B. art. It
C. art, it
D. art: it

40. A. NO CHANGE
B. arts
C. theoretical art
D. theory of art

Name_____ Date_____ Score_____

PRACTICE EXIT EXAM THREE

In Scots history throughout the Highlands, the bagpipes (1) <u>succeeds</u> the harp as a call to arms, especially when the call to arms involved several thousand half-frozen (2) <u>warriors'</u>, most of them out of earshot. The courage of pipers in battle (3) <u>, who were inevitably a prime target,</u> is legendary throughout the centuries. At the Haughs of Cromdale, there's a stone onto which a (4) <u>piper badly-wounded</u> in the Jacobite army climbed and continued to play until he died. The spot is still known as the "Piper's Stone." In the Battle of Philiphaugh, far south in the border country another intrepid piper played until a bullet knocked him into the Ettrick (5) <u>River. Where</u> he drowned.

1. A. NO CHANGE
   B. being succeeded
   C. succeeded
   D. having had succeeded

2. A. NO CHANGE
   B. warriors
   C. warrior's
   D. warrior is

3. A. NO CHANGE
   B. who were inevitably a prime target
   C. – who were inevitably a prime target,
   D. (who were inevitably a prime target)

4. A. NO CHANGE
   B. badly-wounded piper
   C. piper who was badly-wounded
   D. piper who was being wounded badly

5. A. NO CHANGE
   B. River, where
   C. River: where
   D. River, whereas

Perhaps one of the most famous pipers of all (6) are the clan Macdonald's piper who was sent to Duntrune Castle as a herald during a feud during the seventeenth century. He (7) being invited in, but then immediately overpowered and imprisoned. Luckily for the Macdonald clan, the captors neglected to confiscate their prisoner's pipes. Out over the water could soon be heard a sound of pipes resounding an (8) unmistakable and undeniable and distinguishable note of warning. Abruptly the piping stopped as the furious soldiers reached the dungeon and killed (9) them as he played. Although no one knows the real fate of the piper, much later, under the floor of the castle (10) hall; a skeleton was found with mutilated hands.

-Wallace, pp. 44 ;75

6. A. NO CHANGE
   B. to be
   C. were
   D. is

7. A. NO CHANGE
   B. was
   C. were
   D. isn't

8. A. NO CHANGE
   B. note which was unmistakably, undeniably
   C. unmistakably, and then again an undeniably, distinguishable
   D. unmistakable note

9. A. NO CHANGE
   B. the piper
   C. themselves
   D. himself

10. A. NO CHANGE
    B. hall. . .a
    C. hall, a
    D. hall: a

Bulimia is the most common eating disorder in young women. It (11) started as a strategy to control weight, but it develops a life of its own (12) soon. Life for bulimic young women becomes a relentless preoccupation with eating, purging, and weight. Pleasure is replaced by (13) despair, frenzy and guilt. Like all addictions, bulimia is a compulsive, self-destructive and progressive disorder. Binging and purging (14) will be the addictive behaviors; food is the narcotic.

Over time young women with bulimia are at risk for serious health (15) problems; often they have dental problems, esophageal tears, gastrointestinal problems and sometimes dangerous electrolytic imbalances that can trigger heart attacks.

They experience personality changes

11. A. NO CHANGE
    B. has started
    C. will start
    D. starts

12. A. NO CHANGE
    B. insert after "life"
    C. insert after "but"
    D. insert after "develop"

13. A. NO CHANGE
    B. despair frenzy
    C. despair and frenzy
    D. despair; frenzy;

14. A. NO CHANGE
    B. is
    C. are
    D. was

15. A. NO CHANGE
    B. problems
    C. problems –
    D. problems:

As they grow to love binging more than anything else, they become obsessed and (16) secretive.   Driven for another binge and guilty about their habit, (17) The loss of control they experience that leads to depression. Often they are irritable and (18) withdrawn, especially with family members. While anorexia often begins in junior high, bulimia tends to develop in later adolescence. (19) Its called the college girl's disease because so many young women develop it in sororities and dorms.

Estimates of the incidence of bulimia run as high as one-fifth of all college-age women. Most are attractive, with good social skills. Often they are the cheerleaders and homecoming queens, the straight-A students, and the pride of their families. Bulimic young women, like their anorexic sisters are

16. A. NO CHANGE
    B. secretive; driven
    C. secretive, driven
    D. secretive driven

17. A. NO CHANGE
    B. they experience a loss of control
    C. Experience shows them losing control
    D. they experience a control of loss

18. A. NO CHANGE
    B. withdrawing
    C. then they are withdrawing
    D. become withdrawn

19. A. NO CHANGE
    B. Its'
    C. It's
    D. It

oversocialized to the feminine role. They are the (20) people pleasers ultimate.

-Pipher, pp. 169-170

20. A. NO CHANGE
    B. pleasers of people ultimate
    C. people ultimate pleasers
    D. ultimate people pleasers

Earth Medicine is a unique method of personality profiling that draws on Native American understanding of the Universe. (21) He also draws on the principles embodied in sacred medicine wheels. Native Americans believed that (22) spirit although invisible, permeated nature, so that everything in nature was sacred. Animals (23) were perceived as acting as messengers of spirit. If you were born February 29 - March 20, for example, you would be associated with the Wolf. Wolf is the (24) pathfinder. The forerunner of new ideas who returns to share knowledge. Wolf takes one mate for life and is (25) loyally faithful. If you were to keep company with wolves, you would find an enormous sense of family as well as a strong individualistic tendency. The senses of Wolf are very keen, and the moon is its power ally.

21. A. NO CHANGE
    B. She
    C. It
    D. They

22. A. NO CHANGE
    B. spirit, although
    C. spirit; although
    D. spirt (although

23. A. NO CHANGE
    B. could be perceived
    C. are perceived
    D. is perceived

24. A. NO CHANGE
    B. pathfinder, the
    C. pathfinder; the
    D. pathfinder...the

25. A. NO CHANGE
    B. faithfully loyal
    C. loyal
    D. faithfully and loyally

Arthur and Pulley

The moon is the symbol for the unconscious that holds the secrets of knowledge and wisdom. Wolf empowers the teacher within us to come forth and (26) <u>aids</u> the children of Earth in understanding the Great Mystery and (27) <u>life. Individuals</u> associated with the Wolf may wish to share (28) <u>your</u> knowledge by writing or lecturing on information that will help others better understand their uniqueness or path in life. They may also want to (29) <u>out seek lonely places</u> that will allow them to see the teacher within. In (30) <u>aloneness</u> devoid of other humans, an individual may find his or her true self.

-Sams & Carson, pp. 97-98.

26. A. NO CHANGE
    B. aiding
    C. aid
    D. being aided

27. A. NO CHANGE
    B. life; individuals
    C. life – individuals
    D. life. individuals

28. A. NO CHANGE
    B. their
    C. her
    D. there

29. A. NO CHANGE
    B. lonely places seek out
    C. places that are lonely seek out
    D. seek out lonely places

30. A. NO CHANGE
    B. aloneness;
    C. aloneness –
    D. aloneness,

Arthur and Pulley

King James (31) <u>awakes</u> to the sunlight streaming through the casement of his prison cell and (32) <u>laid</u> for a long time reveling in the tranquility. Distant sounds underlined the peace rather than disturbed (33) <u>it and</u> he dozed again before stretching lazily and rising slowly from his bed. Still wrapped in the half-awareness of waking he went to the casement, now without its winter shutters, and leaned out, (34) <u>resting</u> his arms on the ledge.

Below him was a walled and secret (35) <u>garden; closed</u> in with flowering trees, sweet scented in the morning air. He let his eye linger on the blossoms. A robin fluttered into a bough with a flurry of wings and a small movement close under the window attracted his attention.

He caught his breath in the surprise of the (36) <u>moment for</u> seated with

31. A. NO CHANGE
    B. awoke up
    C. awoke
    D. awakening

32. A. NO CHANGE
    B. layed
    C. lie
    D. lay

33. A. NO CHANGE
    B. it, and
    C. it – and
    D. It . . . and

34. A. NO CHANGE
    B. rested
    C. having rested
    D. rests

35. A. NO CHANGE
    B. garden, closed
    C. garden –
    D. garden...closed

36. A. NO CHANGE
    B. moment; for
    C. moment, for
    D. moment –

Arthur and Pulley

abandon on a garden seat was a girl who glowed golden in the sun, the little hat she wore on her abundant hair shining as its beads caught the light. (37) Feathers bright curled downwards over her cheek and shadowed the half-closed eyes but James saw the outline of the cheek and the rounded chin.

How long he watched her he could not afterwards tell, but he feasted his eyes on her beauty, lost in the delight of her being. There seemed about her (38) an aura of well-being and wholesome loveliness. Then, (39) he was gone.

He turned away, trembling, and sat down on his ruffled bed. Here was his golden girl; here was the woman he had searched for down the years. Panic seized him (40) whereas he realized she was no child and might well be claimed already.

-King, pp. 120-121

37. A. NO CHANGE
    B. Bright feathers curled downwards
    C. Curled downwards brightly feathers
    D. Downwards curled bright feathers

38. A. NO CHANGE
    B. an aura that was well-being
    C. a well-being aura
    D. a being-well aura

39. A. NO CHANGE
    B. they
    C. it
    D. she

40. A. NO CHANGE
    B. as if
    C. as
    D. as yet

Name_____ Date_____ Score_____

PRACTICE EXIT EXAM FOUR

From the top of the stairs I had a vantage point into the heart of our home, my mother's kitchen. From there I (1) <u>am</u> to see the terrified face of Chavez when he brought the (2) <u>murderer's terrible news</u> of the sheriff; I was to see the rebellion of my brothers against my (3) <u>father,</u> and many times late at night, I was to see Ultima returning from the plains where she (4) <u>will gather</u> the herbs that can be harvested only in the light of the full moon by the careful hands of a healer.

Ultima slipped easily into the routine of our daily life. My mother was very happy because now she had someone to talk to, and she didn't have to wait until Sunday when her (5) <u>woman</u> friends

1. A. NO CHANGE
   B. to be
   C. was
   D. being

2. A. NO CHANGE
   B. terrible murder news
   C. murder's terrible news
   D. terrible news of the murder

3. A. NO CHANGE
   B. father; and
   C. father–and
   D. father and

4. A. NO CHANGE
   B. gathers
   C. would gather
   D. gathered

5. A. NO CHANGE
   B. women's
   C. women
   D. womens'

Arthur and Pulley

from the town came up the dusty path. Deborah and Theresa were (6) <u>happy. Because</u> Ultima did many of the household chores they normally did. My father was also pleased. Now he had one more person to tell his dream to. (7) <u>It</u> was to gather his sons around him and move westward to the land of the setting sun, to the vineyards of California.

And I was happy with Ultima. We walked together in the plains and (8) <u>into</u> the river banks to gather herbs and roots for her medicines. She taught me the (9) <u>names of</u> plants and flowers, of trees and bushes, of birds and animals; but most importantly, (10) <u>we</u> learned from her that there was a beauty in the time of day and in the time of night, and that there was peace in the river. Her eyes swept the surrounding hills and through them I saw for the first time, the beauty

6. A. NO CHANGE
   B. happy because
   C. happy; because
   D. happy. . .because

7. A. NO CHANGE
   B. His
   C. My father's dream
   D. There

8. A. NO CHANGE
   B. with
   C. at
   D. along

9. A. NO CHANGE
   B. names of:
   C. names of–
   D. names of,

10. A. NO CHANGE
    B. they
    C. he
    D. I

of our hills and the magic of the green

river.

-Anaya, pp. 1;10;13-14

From the rainforests of Costa Rica to the vibrant Maya markets in the Guatemalan (11) highlands. Central America offers endless opportunity to experience and explore. The nations of this narrow (12) isthmus, have emerged from two decades of tumultuous political unrest into a relatively peaceful area– all seven countries (13) had been established democratic governments and crime is decreasing. While Central America has (14) always allured adventurers, increased political stability has expanded the (15) availability of opportunities to budget travelers.

"I'm not going to stay there," you say. 'I'm only going for a couple of weeks." Then it happens. You find that place, that one spot where the scenery is just right: the people are friendly, (16) there are a great hotel with great food, scores

11. A. NO CHANGE
    B. highlands Central
    C. highlands–Central
    D. highlands, Central

12. A. NO CHANGE
    B. isthmus have
    C. isthmus. Have
    D. isthmus; have

13. A. NO CHANGE
    B. had established
    C. had been establishing
    D. have established

14. A. NO CHANGE
    B. insert after "allured"
    C. insert after "adventurers"
    D. omit underlined portion

15. A. NO CHANGE
    B. opportunities available
    C. opportunity availability
    D. available opportunity

16. A. NO CHANGE
    B. their
    C. there is
    D. they are

of fascinating villages nearby await exploration, and a local market with bundles of fresh fruit (17) <u>offers</u> a taste of the good life. These idyllic spots abound in Central America. One such famous site is the Finca Ixobel in Guatemala, where all-you-can-eat dinners, tree-house accommodations, and explorations of the nearby cave system can cast a spell on the wayward traveler. And (18) <u>to</u> entice you even (19) <u>further. Central</u> America offers a system of (20) <u>"volunteering":</u> national parks and wildlife preserves are looking for assistants.

-Let's Go, pp. 1-2

17. A. NO CHANGE
    B. is offering
    C. offered
    D. has offered

18. A. NO CHANGE
    B. omit the underlined portion
    C. two
    D. too

19. A. NO CHANGE
    B. further; Central
    C. further -- Central
    D. further, Central

20. A. NO CHANGE
    B. "volunteering,"
    C. "volunteering"?
    D. "volunteering..."

Arthur and Pulley

The greatest of all the women warriors among the upper Missouri tribes lived among the Crows in the middle of the nineteenth century. Woman Chief was not a Crow Indian by birth. (21) <u>She</u> was a Gros Ventre girl who, at the age of about ten, was captured by the Crows. The Crow family that adopted her soon found that she (22) <u>shown</u> little interest in helping the women with their domestic tasks. She preferred to shoot birds with a bow and arrow, to guard the family horses, and (23) <u>then she wanted to ride</u> horseback fast and fearlessly. Later she learned to shoot a gun (24) <u>accurately. And</u> she became the equal if not the superior of any of the young men in hunting on foot or on horseback.

She grew taller and stronger (25) <u>rather than</u> most women. She could carry a deer home from the hunt on her

21. A. NO CHANGE
    B. This crow
    C. The Woman Chief
    D. The Indian

22. A. NO CHANGE
    B. had shown
    C. had showed
    D. showed

23. A. NO CHANGE
    B. riding
    C. she preferred to ride
    D. to ride

24. A. NO CHANGE
    B. accurately, and
    C. accurately; and
    D. accurately and

25. A. NO CHANGE
    B. then
    C. than
    D. rather

Arthur and Pulley

back. She could kill four buffalo in a single chase, butcher them, and load them on pack horses without assistance. Yet, despite her prowess in men's (26) <u>activities, she</u> always dressed like a woman. Although she was rather (27) <u>good-looking. She</u> didn't attract the fancy of young men. After her foster father died, she took charge of his lodge and family, (28) <u>as both mother and father to his children she acted.</u>

She (29) <u>lead</u> her first war party against the Blackfeet; seventy horses were stolen. She succeeded in killing and scalping one Blackfoot and in capturing the gun of another. Her continued success as a war leader won her greater and greater honors among the Crows until she gained a place in the council of chiefs of the tribe, (30) <u>ranking</u> third in a band of 160 lodges.

-Dorenkamp, et. al, pp. 84-85

26. A. NO CHANGE
    B. activities; she
    C. activities -- she
    D. activities: she

27. A. NO CHANGE
    B. good-looking she
    C. good-looking, she
    D. good-looking -- she

28. A. NO CHANGE
    B. both mother and father acting as his children
    C. acting to his children as both mother and father
    D. acting as both mother and father to his children

29. A. NO CHANGE
    B. led
    C. leaded
    D. leading

30. A. NO CHANGE
    B. however, she ranked
    C. ranked
    D. next ranking

Does an individual always see the same event in the same way? No. The way you see and think about something (31) can change from one moment to the next.

We know that people (32) differed greatly in their ability to absorb stressful situations. (33) Which is often the case in such situations is that you have unknowingly crossed your stress threshold. The ability to absorb stress is not an either you can or you can't proposition. If there were such a thing as a stress (34) meter. To measure this ability on a scale of 1 to 100, you would find people of varied backgrounds at every degree of the scale. (35) Henceforth, if you can decrease the occasions when you cross your stress threshold, you will increase control over some of the events of your life. Fortunately, this is not hard to do.

31. A. NO CHANGE
B. changed
C. has changed
D. would change

32. A. NO CHANGE
B. did differ
C. differs
D. differ

33. A. NO CHANGE
B. What
C. That which
D. Whatever

34. A. NO CHANGE
B. meter, to
C. meter to
D. meter; to

35. A. NO CHANGE
B. In conclusion
C. Therefore
D. For example

It works something like (36) that: say your normal stress threshold rates a 50. Course work, although (37) difficult and challenges, is nothing you can't handle because on a day-to-day basis it offers a stress level of about 30. There are times when the stress of college rises to 45—but you remain relatively calm. (38) Its still below your stress threshold.

Then something happens that lowers your usual stress threshold to 35. You have a grinding headache, or (39) Catie didn't get any sleep the previous night, or you have recently suffered a death in the family. Now those stressful complications in the 40 to 45 range that you customarily handled with ease seem overwhelming. You lose your temper. So to keep your threshold level constant, avoid these vulnerability (40) factors; hunger, anger, substance abuse, loneliness, fatigue, pain, and lack of sleep.

-Freeman & DeWolf, pp. 5; 7; 9.

36. A. NO CHANGE
    B. it
    C. this
    D. stress

37. A. NO CHANGE
    B. challenging
    C. is challenging
    D. has been challenged

38. A. NO CHANGE
    B. Its'
    C. It
    D. It's

39. A. NO CHANGE
    B. he
    C. you
    D. she

40. A. NO CHANGE
    B. factors:
    C. factors,
    D. factors. . .

Name_____ Date_____ Score_____

PRACTICE EXIT EXAM FIVE

For decades, the Australian Aborigines (1) <u>use</u> the boomerang for hunting and warfare. The Aborigines are (2) <u>believe</u> to have developed the returning boomerang, but nonreturning boomerangs were used by hunters in other parts of the world as well. (3) <u>Even</u> North American Indians used a form of nonreturning boomerang.

Today, Australia's returning boomerang has evolved into a (4) <u>plaything. And</u> throwing it has become a sport. There's even a national boomerang throwing championship held annually in New South Wales.

During your travels in Australia you might have an opportunity to learn how to throw a boomerang, and the first thing

1. A. NO CHANGE
   B. used
   C. had used
   D. uses

2. A. NO CHANGE
   B. belief
   C. believes
   D. believed

3. A. NO CHANGE
   B. As if
   C. Although
   D. Unlike

4. A. NO CHANGE
   B. plaything, and
   C. plaything and
   D. Plaything; and

you'll learn is that its' not as easy as it looks. Here are a few tips that might help make your returning boomerang come back as it's supposed to.

(6) First, do your boomerang throwing in a clear, open area. Hold the boomerang vertically (7) by one tip of it, with the flat side of it facing away from you. Bring your arm back behind your head, and then throw the boomerang forward toward the horizon. The trick of a good throw is the snap you give the boomerang as you let it go.

This snap creates a spin that's necessary for the boomerang to gain life. If there's (8) to much (9) lift, though, the boomerang will climb too quickly and eventually plummet to the ground— a good way to break a boomerang. If you've thrown correctly, the boomerang will make a widened circle and then return to you in a horizontal

5. A. NO CHANGE
   B. it
   C. it's
   D. it'll

6. A. NO CHANGE
   B. First; do
   C. First – do
   D. First do

7. A. NO CHANGE
   B. by one of its tips
   C. by its tips of one
   D. its tips of one by it

8. A. NO CHANGE
   B. two
   C. so
   D. too

9. A. NO CHANGE
   B. lift though, the
   C. lift, though the
   D. lift; though, the

position. As it nears you, it may make several more small spins, or hover before it lands near your feet. A skilled boomerang thrower can send a boomerang into a 50-yard-wide circle before (10) <u>he</u> returns.

    If you don't succeed the first time, keep practicing, remembering that it's the snap that counts.

-Erickson, p. 120

10. A. NO CHANGE
     B. you
     C. it
     D. itself

Arthur and Pulley

Most of my (11) <u>memories of important moments</u> with Peter center in an old black Ford. One balmy summer evening I remember particularly. Emily and Ted were out cruising in his rusty two-tone (12) <u>Chevy, the</u> lawyer's son, Jim, and his girl had his father's shiny Buick, and Peter and I were out driving in the Ford. As we (13) <u>rumble</u> slowly down Main Street, quiet and dark at night, Peter saw Ted's car (14) <u>approached</u>. We stopped in the middle of the street. One of us suggested that we all meet later at a (15) <u>park of woods</u> a few miles north of town. An hour or so (16) <u>later. Peter</u> and I bumped over the potholes in the road that twisted through the woods to the parking lot. (17) <u>They</u> were the first ones there.

It was so quiet, I was a little

11. A. NO CHANGE
    B. memories of moments that are important
    C. important memories being moments
    D. moments having been important memories

12. A. NO CHANGE
    B. Chevy; the
    C. Chevy – the
    D. Chevy. The

13. A. NO CHANGE
    B. rumbles
    C. had rumbled
    D. rumbled

14. A. NO CHANGED
    B. approaches
    C. approaching
    D. has approached

15. A. NO CHANGE
    B. parkwood
    C. wood park
    D. wooded park

16. A. NO CHANGE
    B. later, Peter
    C. later; Peter
    D. later...Peter

17. A. NO CHANGE
    B. Ourselves
    C. We
    D. He and she

Arthur and Pulley

(18) <u>frightening</u>, thinking of warnings about dangerous men who sometimes preyed upon couples in secluded places.

(19) <u>Consequently</u>, we simply sat and talked, with Peter's arm draped casually on the back of the seat. Gradually I moved a little closer. My sixteenth birthday was only a few weeks away, and so far I had nothing substantial to report. For many years I never told anyone about what did happen to me that first time. I was too ashamed.

During a silence I turned my face toward him, and then he kissed me, quickly. I was (20) <u>exhilarated, but</u> frightened. I wanted to respond, but my instincts did not entirely cooperate. I leaned toward Peter, but at the last moment I panicked. Instead of kissing him, I gave him a sudden lick on the cheek. He didn't know what to say.

-Olson-Fallon, pp. 69-70

18. A. NO CHANGE
    B. fright
    C. of fright
    D. frightened

19. A. NO CHANGE
    B. Therefore
    C. However
    D. For a while

20. A. NO CHANGE
    B. exhilarated but
    C. exhilarated; but
    D. exhilarated. But

Pyramids did not stand alone but were part of a group of buildings which included temples, chapels, (21) mummies in other tombs, and massive walls. Remnants of funerary boats have been excavated; the best preserved is at Giza. On the walls of Fifth and Sixth Dynasty pyramids are inscriptions known as the Pyramid (22) Texts. . . an important source of information about Egyptian religion. The (23) ancient records scarcity, however, makes uncertain the uses of all the buildings in the pyramid complex or the exact burial procedures. It is thought that the (24) kings body was brought by boat up the Nile to the pyramid site and probably (25) having been mummified in the Valley Temple before being placed in the pyramid for burial.

The funerary customs and beliefs of

21. A. NO CHANGE
    B. mummies
    C. other tombs
    D. mummification

22. A. NO CHANGE
    B. Texts an
    C. Texts; an
    D. Texts, an

23. A. NO CHANGE
    B. ancient records and scarcity
    C. scarcity of ancient records
    D. records of ancient scarcity

24. A. NO CHANGE
    B. king
    C. king's
    D. kings'

25. A. NO CHANGE
    B. mummified
    C. mummifies
    D. mummifying

the ancient Egyptians called for the preservation of the body and ample provisions for the afterlife. This was envisioned as a continuation of the existence before death. An ancient Egyptian (26) will provide for the life in the next World as best as he could. For us today, this means that a huge amount of information about daily life in ancient Egypt can be found in the tombs. Detailed and colorful scenes on the walls provide information on a wide range of (27) topics dress, agriculture, architecture, crafts, and food (28) production. And the goods included in the tomb along with the corpse add to this information resource.

    The Egyptians painted idealized scenes from daily life: scenes of agricultural work such as crop

26. A. NO CHANGE
    B. is providing
    C. should be providing
    D. provided

27. A. NO CHANGE
    B. topics: dress
    C. topics, dress
    D. topics; dress

28. A. NO CHANGE
    B. production; and
    C. production. The
    D. production – and

Arthur and Pulley

harvesting, cattle tending, and (29) fishing. (30) It illustrated scenes of artisans at their work, including gold workers and boat-builders. These scenes represented the hoped for after-life and were thought to ensure an ideal existence in the next world.

-O'brien

29. A. NO CHANGE
B. fish
C. fishes
D. gone fishing

30. A. NO CHANGE
B. It's
C. She
D. They

Arthur and Pulley

When I took my first job out of college, working as a legislative aide on Capitol Hill, I finally (31) have met the man of my childhood dreams. (32) No, not the knight in shining armor I hoped to marry someday, but the big brother I'd always dreamed of having.

John and I worked for the same (33) congressman we shared an office. (34) Previously, two-thirds of our waking hours were spent together, and we became very good friends. (35) Whereas a political neophyte, I often turned to him for advice in my job, and soon I sought his counsel on other matters as well. It was John who (36) had took me shopping for my first car, prodded me into learning basic household repairs, and coached me on the fine art of asking for a raise. In turn, I helped John shop for his suits, protectively passed judgment on the various women in his

31. A. NO CHANGE
    B. met
    C. had been meeting
    D. had met

32. A. NO CHANGE
    B. No not
    C. No; not
    D. No. Not

33. A. NO CHANGE
    B. congressman;
    C. congressman – we
    D. congressman, we

34. A. NO CHANGE
    B. For instance
    C. Next
    D. Consequently

35. A. NO CHANGE
    B. Meanwhile
    C. Because of
    D. As

36. A. NO CHANGE
    B. taking
    C. should take
    D. took

life, and (37) <u>then I provided</u> an amused ear the night he practically came (38) <u>unglued. After</u> shaking hands with the Vice President of the United States.

Such opposite-sex friendships are increasingly common. Researchers say these friendships contribute to (39) <u>happier, and</u> healthier lives for those involved. Men as well as women (40) <u>often</u> search for the warmth and intimacy of a platonic friendship. In fact, the research of Dean and Lin revealed that more men had opposite-sex friendships than women.

-Bender & Leone, pp. 208-209

37. A. NO CHANGE
    B. provided
    C. having had provided
    D. then I had provided

38. A. NO CHANGE
    B. unglued, after
    C. unglued after
    D. unglued; after

39. A. NO CHANGE
    B. happier and
    C. happier; and
    D. happier healthier

40. A. NO CHANGE
    B. insert after "Men"
    C. insert after "friendship"
    D. insert after "intimacy"

Name_____ Date_____ Score_____

PRACTICE EXIT EXAM SIX

Arthur Ashe was one of the first African-Americans to become a great tennis champion. After a heart attack (1) end his career, he contracted AIDS through a tainted blood transfusion. While he pursued many business interests and human rights (2) projects he kept his illness private for years. Then the possibility of a newspaper report forced him to reveal his condition to the public by way of a press conference held in April, 1992.

The day after the press (3) conference Ashe made sure he kept the two appointments on his calendar (4) because he was anxious to see how people would respond to (5) Ashe after the announcement. He was thinking

1. A. NO CHANGE
   B. has ended
   C. could end
   D. ended

2. A. NO CHANGE
   B. projects, he
   C. projects. He
   D. projects; he

3. A. NO CHANGE
   B. conference, Ashe
   C. conference – Ashe
   D. conference; Ashe

4. A. NO CHANGE
   B. yet
   C. being that
   D. for example

5. A. NO CHANGE
   B. he
   C. hisself
   D. him

Arthur and Pulley

not only about the people he knew personally, even intimately, but also about waiters and bartenders, doormen and (6) <u>driving taxis</u>. He knew all the myths and fears about AIDS. He also understood that if he hadn't contracted the disease and lived with it, he would probably share some of those myths and fears. He knew that he couldn't spread the disease by (7) <u>coughing, breath,</u> or using cups in a restaurant, but he knew that in some places his cups would receive some extra soap and hot water or be smashed and thrown away.

    Ashe was glad that eventually he (8) <u>stopped to conceal</u> his condition from certain people. He had reminded himself from the outset that he had an obligation to tell anyone who might be materially or personally hurt by the news when it came out. Not one of the companies, not even Home Box Office (HBO)

6. A. NO CHANGE
   B. taxis that were driven by men
   C. drivers who taxied
   D. taxi drivers

7. A. NO CHANGE
   B. coughing, breathing
   C. his cough, breath
   D. the cough, breathing

8. A. NO CHANGE
   B. concealed stopping
   C. stopped concealing
   D. stopped to concealment

(9) he was a spokesperson for dropped him after he quietly revealed that he had AIDS. He waited for the phone calls and the signs that his services were no longer needed. (10) None came.

Ashe died on February 6, 1993.

-Fawcett & Sandberg, pp. 506-508

9. A. NO CHANGE
   B. a spokesperson for which he was
   C. for which he was a spokesperson
   D. which for a spokesperson he was

10. A. NO CHANGE
    B. Nobody came.
    C. It didn't come.
    D. None came around to him.

Basic to the Japanese tradition of Shinto are (11) spirits called "Kami." Spirits are located in specific places in the empirical (12) world. In a temple, in a (13) crib, or in a shrine. One of the Japanese estimates (14) are that there are eight million kami. This term refers both to the sense of power felt in things of the world and to particular spirits. A waterfall is a powerful spirit, (15) in contrast designating it communicates the sense an observer has of its immense power.

Perhaps the most important spirits are those in the house. They occupy particular places and protect the members of the household when in those places: the god of the kitchen lives in the kitchen, the bathroom god in the bathroom, and so forth. (16) There is also a guardian deity of the household. This spirit is made up of

11. A. NO CHANGE
    B. spirits; called
    C. spirits, called
    D. spirits. Called

12. A. NO CHANGE
    B. world, in
    C. world: in
    D. world in

13. A. NO CHANGE
    B. suitcase
    C. car
    D. house

14. A. NO CHANGE
    B. is
    C. being
    D. were

15. A. NO CHANGE
    B. however
    C. nonetheless
    D. so

16. A. NO CHANGE
    B. They're
    C. Their
    D. There are

many ancestors who have merged to guard the house as a corporate unit that exists over time. The village has a guardian deity, often a fox god or an ancestor of a founding member. Villagers (17) asking the village god for help in their rice (18) harvest, or for success in schooling.

People (19) creating new kami as needed. In a less individuated way, all equipment, from computer chips to cameras to automobile production machinery, are thought to have a spiritual side. In 1990 engineers met at Tokyo's Chomeiji shrine (20) for the service their used-up equipment had given them to thank it.

-Bowen, pp. 29-30

17. A. NO CHANGE
    B. ask
    C. would ask
    D. asked

18. A. NO CHANGE
    B. harvest. Or
    C. Harvest; or
    D. harvest or

19. A. NO CHANGE
    B. creates
    C. create
    D. having to create

20. A. NO CHANGE
    B. for to thank their equipment that was used-up for its service to them.
    C. to thank it, the equipment that was used-up for the service it had given them.
    D. to thank their used-up equipment for the service it had given them.

Technological advance in our society has been accompanied by a quantity of challenges to our bodies and our (21) health. The ability to change (22) your looks and our bodily processes with a pill or an implant causes an overload on our (23) immunity systems that can produce a type of condition called environmental illness. Another cause of environmental illness is potentially carcinogenic types of microscopic pollution in our air, water, homes, and (24) workable places. Generally speaking, women (25) tending to be more prone to environmental illness than men. This is in part because a number of chemical toxins actually mimic estrogen in the body, causing (26) in the hormone an insufficiency.

Dr. Silverman says that thousands of

21. A. NO CHANGE
    B. healthful.
    C. health living.
    D. healthiness.

22. A. NO CHANGE
    B. their
    C. our
    D. man's

23. A. NO CHANGE
    B. immune
    C. immature
    D. immaturity

24. A. NO CHANGE
    B. places where everyday people work
    C. places that are working
    D. workplaces

25. A. NO CHANGE
    B. tend
    C. had tended
    D. has tended

26. A. NO CHANGE
    B. in the hormone causing an insufficiency
    C. in the hormonal insufficiency
    D. an insufficiency in the hormone

poisons in our (27) food. Water and surroundings are responsible for environmental illness: "The first thing you must realize is that what you eat can have a tremendous effect on your immune system. One of the most toxic foods that people expose themselves to unknowingly, for example, (28) are hydrogenated (29) oil people don't realize how widespread that ingredient is. It's in crackers, all commercial breads, potato chips, pretzels, and cookies; and it has a very strong damaging effect on the immune system.

Along with what you eat, you must consider what you drink. Most people are being exposed to tap water, whether directly from their sink or outside when they buy a cup of coffee. Probably one of the highest exposures to cancer causing agents (30) comes from this source.   -Null, p. 157

27. A. NO CHANGE
    B. food water
    C. food, water,
    D. food and water

28. A. NO CHANGE
    B. is
    C. were
    D. was

29. A. NO CHANGE
    B. oil; People
    C. oil – people
    D. oil. People

30. A. NO CHANGE
    B. come
    C. is coming
    D. have come

Most serfs were born, (31) and the serfs lived, and died on the same manor, very provincial and limited in their outlook. (32) Later, if a runaway serf escaped to a town without being caught for a year and a day, he could gain his freedom and become a (33) man who is freed up.

In terms of creature comforts, the serfs' lives were miserable by (34) quite our standards. Adults, children, and, in the winter, farm (35) infestations of animals with bugs and fleas lived in a one-room thatched hut. The hut often had a dirt floor and a hole in the roof for a chimney. In this crowded environment, accidents, disease, and malnutrition often took their toll, (36) reduce the expectancy of living to thirty or forty years. The overworked peasants had meat only a few times a year, usually at

31. A. NO CHANGE
    B. born, lived, and died
    C. born, lived, and the serfs died
    D. being born, lived, and died

32. A. NO CHANGE
    B. Later if
    C. Later – if
    D. Later; if

33. A. NO CHANGE
    B. freeman
    C. man of freedom
    D. man who is being set free

34. A. NO CHANGE
    B. insert after "lives"
    C. insert after "were"
    D. insert after "standards"

35. A. NO CHANGE
    B. bugs and fleas infested with animals
    C. infestations of bugs and fleas on animals
    D. animals infested with bugs and fleas

36. A. NO CHANGE
    B. reducing
    C. reduced
    D. reduces

Arthur and Pulley

Christmas, Easter, (37) and at the Pentecost. Their everyday fare was the perpetual cabbage soup, grain bread, and maybe cheese and ale for dinner. Not aware of the germ theory of (38) disease. Medieval serfs rarely (39) had washed their utensils or their hands.

Serfs turned over one-tenth of their produce to the church. Each serf worked perhaps three days a week for the lord and one day for the church, (40) leaving him two days for himself and his family.

-Keboe, et. al., p. 319

37. A. NO CHANGE
B. and then at Pentecost
C. and Pentecost
D. then at Pentecost

38. A. NO CHANGE
B. disease: medieval
C. disease medieval
D. disease, medieval

39. A. NO CHANGE
B. has washed
C. washed
D. wash

40. A. NO CHANGE
B. having left him two days
C. having left over two days for him
D. being left him two days

PRACTICE EXIT EXAM SEVEN

All Arab governments now strongly (1) supports efforts to increase women's educational opportunities. In 1956, many years before the issue gained its current (2) prominence. The Tunisian President, Habib Bourguiba, instituted laws improving the legal status of women and ultimately became known as "Liberator of Women." Iraq revised personal status laws regarding marriage, child (3) custody, and inheritance in 1959. Egypt has drastically revised laws concerning marriage and divorce; for example, an Egyptian woman can now (4) pursue for divorce if her husband takes a second wife without her permission. In Morocco a woman can stipulate in (5) herself marriage contract

1. A. NO CHANGE
   B. support
   C. has support
   D. is supporting

2. A. NO CHANGE
   B. prominence the
   C. prominence, the
   D. prominence—the

3. A. NO CHANGE
   B. custody, and some inheritance
   C. custody, and also inheritance
   D. custody, and then Iraq revised inheritance

4. A. NO CHANGE
   B. suit
   C. sue
   D. pursuant

5. A. NO CHANGE
   B. she
   C. the woman's
   D. her

that polygamy is grounds for divorce. In the past ten to twenty years, personal status laws have been revised to increase the legal rights of women in most Arab countries, either by supplementing or (6) <u>they reinterpret</u> traditional Islamic law. In virtually every Arab country (7) <u>today, the</u> laws regarding women are being discussed and are imminently subject to change.

   (8) <u>Do not let it be assuming</u> that (9) <u>being that</u> the role of Arab women is not highly visible in public, their influence is similarly diminished in private life. In traditional Arab society, men and women have well-defined spheres of activity and influence. Men are responsible for providing for the family's material welfare. Even if a woman has money, she need not contribute to family expenses. Most women in fact do have their own money, and Islamic religious

6. A. NO CHANGE
   B. reinterpreting
   C. having
   D. is

7. A. NO CHANGE
   B. today the
   C. today: the
   D. today; the

8. A. NO CHANGE
   B. Do not be assuming
   C. Do not assume
   D. Assume, do not do it

9. A. NO CHANGE
   B. for
   C. because
   D. nevertheless

law (10) <u>states, clearly</u> that they retain

sole control over the women's money

and inheritance after marriage.

-Nydell, p. 54

10. A. NO CHANGE
    B. states clearly
    C. states; clearly
    D. states. Clearly

Arthur and Pulley — Page 144

Television images haunt (11) us. Stunted, bony bodies. This is hunger in its acute form.

But hunger comes in another form. It is the day-to-day hunger that over 700 million people suffer. Every year this (12) hunger, largely invisible, kills as many as 20 million people.

So we ask ourselves, what really is hunger? Is it the physical depletion of those suffering chronic undernutrition? Yes, but it is more.

As long as we (13) have a hunger conception only in physical measures, we will never truly understand it, certainly not (14) it's roots. What would it mean to think of hunger in terms of (15) emotions human and universal? We'll give you an idea of what we mean.

Dr. Clements writes of a family in El Salvador he tried to help whose son and daughter had died. "Both had been lost

11. A. NO CHANGE
    B. us: stunted, bony
    C. us; stunted, bony
    D. us, stunted, bony

12. A. NO CHANGE
    B. large hunger that is invisible
    C. hunger large and invisible
    D. hunger that's invisibly enlarged

13. A. NO CHANGE
    B. are of the conception of hunger
    C. have a conceiving hunger
    D. conceive of hunger

14. A. NO CHANGE
    B. its
    C. its'
    D. is it

15. A. NO CHANGE
    B. universally human emotions
    C. human emotions that are universal
    D. universal human emotions

Arthur and Pulley

when Camila and her husband (16) having chosen to pay their mortgage rather than keep the money to feed their children. Thus, being hungry means (17) *anguish. The* anguish of impossible choices.

In Nicaragua four years ago, we met Amanda Espinoza who never had enough to feed her family. She had endured six stillbirths and (18) then Amanda watched five of her children die before the age of one. To Amanda, hunger means *grief*.

Walking into a home in the rural Philippines, the first words the doctor heard (19) was an apology for the poverty of the dwelling. Being hungry also means living in *humiliation*.

In Guatemala in 1978, we learned that one of two men we had met had been forced into hiding; the other had been killed. For the wealthy, the men's crime

16. A. NO CHANGE
    B. have chose
    C. chosen
    D. had chosen

17. A. NO CHANGE
    B. anguish the
    C. anguish; the
    D. anguish: the

18. A. NO CHANGE
    B. she was watching
    C. watched
    D. then watching

19. A. NO CHANGE
    B. were
    C. are
    D. is

was teaching their neighbors better farming techniques. Guatemala's wealthy feel threatened by any change that makes the poor less dependent on jobs on their rich plantations. Lastly, (20) <u>than,</u> a dimension of hunger is *fear*.

-Lappe & Collins, pp. 2-4

20. A. NO CHANGE
    B. that
    C. thus
    D. then

Arthur and Pulley

(In the Barnyard)

Wilbur liked Charlotte the spider better and better each day. Her campaign against insects seemed sensible, and (21) she made use of it. Wilbur admired the way Charlotte managed. He was (22) partially glad that she always put her victim to sleep before eating (23) them.

As the days went by, Wilbur grew and grew. He ate three big meals a day. (24) The humans ate three big meals a day, too. He spent long hours lying on his side, half asleep, dreaming pleasant dreams. He enjoyed good (25) health and he gained a lot of weight. One afternoon the oldest sheep walked into the barn and stopped to pay a call on Wilbur.

"Hello!" she said. "It seems to me you're putting on weight."

"Yes, I guess I am," replied Wilbur.

21. A. NO CHANGE
    B. useful
    C. using
    D. usefulness

22. A. NO CHANGE
    B. particularly
    C. peculiarly
    D. in particular

23. A. NO CHANGE
    B. him
    C. herself
    D. it

24. A. NO CHANGE
    B. omit the underlined portion
    C. Humans eat three meals a day, too.
    D. Humans eat meals, too, you know.

25. A. NO CHANGE
    B. health; and
    C. health, and
    D. health: and

Arthur and Pulley   Page 148

"At my age it's a good idea to keep gaining."

"Just the same, I don't envy you. You know why they're fattening you (26) up; don't you?"

26. A. NO CHANGE
    B. up don't
    C. up, don't
    D. up, do not

"No," said Wilbur.

"Well, I don't like to spread bad news," said the sheep, "but (27) there going to kill you !"

27. A. NO CHANGE
    B. they're
    C. their
    D. omit the underlined portion

"Save (28) myself, somebody! Save me!"

28. A. NO CHANGE
    B. Wilbur
    C. me
    D. him

"Be quiet, Wilbur," said Charlotte who had been listening to this awful conversation.

"I can't be quiet. I don't want to be killed. Is it true what the old sheep says, Charlotte?" screamed Wilbur.

"The old sheep has been around this barn a long time. I'm sure it's true. It's also the dirtiest trick I ever heard of."

Wilbur (29) burst into tears.

29. A. NO CHANGE
    B. bursted
    C. bust
    D. busted

"You shall not die," said Charlotte,

briskly.

"What? Really? (30) <u>Who</u> going to save me?"

"I am," said Charlotte.

-White, pp. 48-51

30. A. NO CHANGE
    B. Who're
    C. Whose
    D. Who's

Arthur and Pulley

In 1781, (31) the slave, Elizabeth Freeman, also called "Mum Bett," sued for her freedom. Born in 1742 to African slaves in Claverack, New York, (32) the slave was purchased from a Mr. Hodgeboom when she was six months old by her new owner, Colonel Ashley of Sheffield, Massachusetts. She (33) serves as his house servant through middle age. When the master's wife in a (34) rage of fit went to strike Mum Bett's sister, Mum Bett received the blow instead. Injured, she left her (35) master house and refused to return. When her master appealed to the court for her recovery in 1781, she sought the help of a (36) lawyer that was young, Theodore Sedgwick of nearby Stockbridge. During the years of the Revolution, she had heard discussions about the Declaration of Rights (1780) in the Massachusetts (37) Constitution, and told the young

31. A. NO CHANGE
    B. the slave of Elizabeth
    C. the slave person of Elizabeth
    D. the person who was the slave Elizabeth

32. A. NO CHANGE
    B. she
    C. this slave
    D. the woman

33. A. NO CHANGE
    B. did serve
    C. served
    D. was serving

34. A. NO CHANGE
    B. fitted rage
    C. rage fit
    D. fit of rage

35. A. NO CHANGE
    B. master's
    C. masters
    D. omit the underlined portion

36. A. NO CHANGE
    B. lawyer that was youthful
    C. young lawyer
    D. lawyer who was very young

37. A. NO CHANGE
    B. Constitution. And
    C. Constitution and
    D. Constitution; and

Arthur and Pulley

lawyer that those rights certainly must apply to her since she was not a "dumb beast." Sedgwick argued the case for her and another of Ashley's slaves, Brom. Both slaves won their freedom, and Ashley had to pay the cost for court.

(38) <u>Although Ashley offered her wages to return,</u> she went to work for the Sedgwicks as their housekeeper, protecting their house from vandals during Shay's Rebellion in late 1786. She became a respected nurse and (39) <u>was a midwife who delivered babies</u> after she moved in with her daughter, "Little (40) Bett". With whom she lived through the War of 1812 until her death in 1829.

-Salem, p. 87

38. A good beginning for the last paragraph would be

  A. NO CHANGE
  B. When Ashley apologized and gave her money,
  C. Elizabeth never again got wages.
  D. Because Ashley offered her wages to return,

39. A. NO CHANGE
  B. midwife
  C. then she was a midwife
  D. a nurse who delivered babies

40. A. NO CHANGE
  B. Bett"; with
  C. Bett," with
  D. Bett": with

Name_____ Date_____ Score_____

PRACTICE EXIT EXAM EIGHT

We (1) <u>have find</u> that different nonverbal signals are used in various cities. Understanding the fact that there are differences can keep one out of (2) <u>situations that are so embarrassing</u>. Recently, while flying from Atlanta to New York, we encountered this factor in a discussion with a very gracious (3) <u>chick of the South's descent</u>. She disliked going to New York City because of the supposed indifference that people displayed toward others. "Moreover," she said, "I (4) <u>especially</u> don't enjoy not being looked at and (5) <u>when I am</u> made to feel that I don't exist. Why, in the South, we take the time to look at people and, as you know, smile at them."

1. A. NO CHANGE
   B. have founded
   C. have found
   D. finding

2. A. NO CHANGE
   B. situations that could lead on to become embarrassing
   C. embarrassing situations
   D. situations of embarrassment

3. A. NO CHANGE
   B. southern lady
   C. lady from the southern region
   D. lady who was from the South

4. A. NO CHANGE
   B. insert before Moreover
   C. insert after enjoy
   D. insert after at

5. A. NO CHANGE
   B. also when I am
   C. being
   D. neither when I'm

(Indeed it has been observed that Peachtree Street in Atlanta is a location where one is smiled at very often.) We explained that individuals' nonverbal signals vary from city to city and section to section.

In densely populated areas such as (6) New York City, and Tokyo, people give the impression that they are disregarding one (7) another a newcomer might (8) have took their gestures to mean complete indifference. Yet studies conducted to determine how people in crowded cities react during a time of crisis—such as the 1965 New York power blackout—(9) reveals that an overwhelming majority respond by helping others in need. These "good Samaritans" with hard-shell exteriors show their true colors at such times. In less densely populated areas where individuals depend on each other more

6. A. NO CHANGE
   B. New York City; and Tokyo
   C. New York City; and Tokyo
   D. New York City (and Tokyo)

7. A. NO CHANGE
   B. another. A
   C. another: a
   D. another

8. A. NO CHANGE
   B. took
   C. could have taken
   D. take

9. A. NO CHANGE
   B. has revealing
   C. have reveals
   D. reveal

and Southern hospitality prevails, signals such as smiles, winks, and a warm "Hey" are commonplace. A New Yorker, however, would probably be taken (10) <u>aback. If</u> greeted in this manner by a stranger.

-Nierenberg & Calero, pp. 140-141

10. A. NO CHANGE
B. aback; if
C. aback, if
D. aback if

Arthur and Pulley Page 156

Conrad Hilton started with only a dream – no money – just a (11) big, big dream. But he did what most people are not willing to do. He added (12) action, and turned his imagination into a plan. He gave the plan details, scheduled the details, and (13) he made alternate plans in case the first plan failed. Most importantly, he put his plan into action and made it (14) come all altogether and come true. If you don't dream big, you certainly won't achieve much. It is against the basic laws that govern (15) man unless you can visualize something, you cannot attain it.

Amazing as it sounds, the great majority of people in the United States don't spend even an hour a week, pencil in hand, planning a strategy for their financial future. (16) He once said, "Most people are so busy earning a living, they never make any money."

11. A. NO CHANGE
 B. big big
 C. big; big
 D. big – big

12. A. NO CHANGE
 B. action and
 C. action. And
 D. omit underlined portion

13. A. NO CHANGE
 B. then he made
 C. and then making
 D. made

14. A. NO CHANGE
 B. come fully true altogether
 C. come true
 D. come true altogether

15. A. NO CHANGE
 B. man, unless
 C. man. Unless
 D. man...unless

16. A. NO CHANGE
 B. They
 C. Anybody
 D. Someone

Arthur and Pulley

And it's true!

-Haroldsen, p. 16

(17) <u>As soon as</u> the typical American has a small amount of money saved, he is tempted to spend it on depreciating assets such as cars, (18) <u>camping</u>, boats, or trailers. Most spend their entire lives saving just enough to buy something to keep up with their neighbors. They never have enough (19) <u>to make any left over, meaningful investments</u>.

To belong to that exclusive group of millionaires, the one out of a thousand, you must begin by following the rule of 10%. Any increase in the 10% rule speeds you on the way to making your fortune. The 10% rule is a simple one, but a difficult one for some to follow. You must save a minimum of 10% of your gross (20) <u>earnings the</u> second part of the rule is that you never, never spend that savings!

17. A. NO CHANGE
    B. For when
    C. Next,
    D. However,

18. A. NO CHANGE
    B. campers
    C. camping out
    D. outback camps

19. A. NO CHANGE
    B. for any meaningful investment left over
    C. for investments meaningfully left over
    D. left over to make any meaningful investments

20. A. NO CHANGE
    B. earnings, the
    C. earnings. The
    D. earnings...the

Arthur and Pulley

They were hoping for a son. It was a daughter. The future Catherine II of Russia was born at Stettin on April 21, 1729. (21) It was given the names Sophie Augusta Fredericka. The young mother, Johanna Elizabeth, was distressed that she had not been able to produce a (22) boy. And spent little time watching over the cradle. Johanna was convinced that with her beauty and worldly wisdom she could have achieved a higher (23) destiny instead of the brilliant rise she (24) has once dreamed of, (25) for example, she had to be content with a husband of modest position. It was her family who had arranged the match, (26) consulting without her. At fifteen, she had married Prince Christian Augustus, a man twenty-seven years her senior. Truly a person of no great importance, he was one of those obscure princes in the

21. A. NO CHANGE
    B. She
    C. That child
    D. Theirs

22. A. NO CHANGE
    B. boy, and
    C. boy; and
    D. boy and

23. A. NO CHANGE
    B. destiny...instead
    C. destiny. Instead
    D. destiny, instead

24. A. NO CHANGE
    B. having
    C. would
    D. had

25. A. NO CHANGE
    B. however
    C. thus
    D. so

26. A. NO CHANGE
    B. consulted
    C. having been consulted
    D. had consulted

fragmented Germany of the eighteenth century. Her husband was a major general in the Prussian army. This worthy man, devoted to (27) <u>order,</u> thrift, and religion, surrounded Johanna with affection, but that was far from enough to satisfy her. She had a passion for worldly intrigue and chafed at holding so poor a place in society. (28) <u>Fortunately</u> shortly after Sophie was born, the family was able to move into the fortified castle of Stettin. It was a small promotion. The following year, another piece of good (29) <u>fortune Johanna</u> at last gave birth to a boy. God had heard her prayers! She lavished the affection and pride she had denied her daughter upon the infant. Sophie, still very young, suffered bitterly from (30) <u>the preference of her mother</u> for the newcomer.

-Troyat, pp. 1-2

27. A. NO CHANGE
    B. order and
    C. order, and
    D. order, and also

28. A. NO CHANGE
    B. Fortunately–
    C. Fortunately,
    D. Fortunately;

29. A. NO CHANGE
    B. fortune: Johanna
    C. fortune, Johanna
    D. fortune...Johanna

30. A. NO CHANGE
    B. preferred preference of her mother
    C. preference by her mother
    D. her mother's preference

By 1899, several issues moved social reformers to institute a juvenile court in Chicago. Prosecutors attempted to hold youthful offenders between the ages of seven and 14 responsible for their crimes as (31) adults if convicted, such juveniles would be incarcerated with an adult prison population and, in 10 cases before 1900, even executed.

(32) Consequently, in 1899 Illinois legislation gave courts jurisdiction over juveniles charged with crimes and over (33) children's who were neglected. The purpose was stated as rehabilitation (34) on the other hand than punishment. It also provided for the confidentiality of the youthful offender's records. In another protective step, the act has required the separation of juveniles from adults when incarcerated and (35) barred the detention of juveniles under 12 in jails altogether.

31. A. NO CHANGE
    B. adults, if
    C. adults. If
    D. adults (if

32. A. NO CHANGE
    B. Because
    C. Whereas
    D. In spite of it

33. A. NO CHANGE
    B. childrens
    C. children
    D. childrens'

34. A. NO CHANGE
    B. rather than
    C. as
    D. nonetheless

35. A. NO CHANGE
    B. barring
    C. did bar
    D. having barred

In addition to providing for public safety and (36) having removed perpetrators from the (37) community, the juvenile justice system remains a part of the promise that communities (38) makes to youth. Courts examine the roles of family, schools, neighborhoods, and (39) then they examine social services in the lives of (40) juveniles, they make an effort to restore the fundamental promise of youth as a time of development in caring and nurturing environments.

-Couto & Stutts, pp. 17

36. A. NO CHANGE
    B. removes
    C. removing
    D. being removed

37. A. NO CHANGE
    B. community; the
    C. community. The
    D. community the

38. A. NO CHANGE
    B. would make
    C. making
    D. make

39. A. NO CHANGE
    B. servicing socials
    C. examinations of social services
    D. social services

40. A. NO CHANGE
    B. juveniles; they
    C. juveniles. They
    D. juveniles they

PRACTICE EXIT EXAM NINE

The reforms and foreign policy of King Mongut (1) was carried out by his son and successor. King Rama V of Thailand came to the throne as a frail youth of sixteen and died one of Siam's most loved and revered kings. He had a remarkable reign of 42 (2) years indeed, modern Thailand (3) may be said it could be a product of the comprehensive and (4) progressing reforms of his reign. For these touched almost every aspect of Thai life.

King Rama V faced the Western world with a (5) positive, and eager attitude: eager to learn about Western ideas and inventions, positively working towards Western-style "progress" while at the same time (6) resisted Western

1. A. NO CHANGE
   B. were
   C. wasn't
   D. isn't

2. A. NO CHANGE
   B. years, indeed
   C. years - indeed
   D. years. Indeed

3. A. NO CHANGE
   B. may be said to be
   C. maybe it could be said
   D. maybe it could be said to be

4. A. NO CHANGE
   B. progress
   C. progressive
   D. progressed

5. A. NO CHANGE
   B. positive and eager
   C. positive; and eager
   D. positive (and eager)

6. A. NO CHANGE
   B. and resists
   C. also resisting
   D. resisting

(7) rule he was the first Thai king to travel abroad; he did not just travel as an observer or tourist but worked hard during his trips to further Thai interests.

The King also traveled within his own country. He was passionately interested in his (8) subjects welfare and was intent on the monarchy assuming a more visible role in society. He wanted to see how his subjects lived and went outside his palace often, sometimes incognito. His progressive outlook led him to his first official act, forbidding prostration in the royal presence. He gradually abolished the institution of slavery, a (9) momentous and positive change for Thai society.

With so many achievements to his credit and a charisma that was enhanced by his longevity, it was no wonder that the Thai people grieved long and genuinely for King Rama V when he

7. A. NO CHANGE
   B. rule—he
   C. rule. He
   D. rule; he

8. A. NO CHANGE
   B. subject's
   C. subjects'
   D. subjects are

9. A. NO CHANGE
   B. momentously positive change
   C. change momentously positive
   D. positively momentous changing

died. October 23, the date of his death, is still a (10) holiday that's national, in honor of one of Siam's greatest and most beloved kings.

-Office of the Prime Minister, 1991

10. A. NO CHANGE
    B. nationalized holiday
    C. holiday national
    D. national holiday

Arthur and Pulley

Are rituals, activities, (11) <u>and games</u> always bad in a relationship? It is safe to say that games nearly always (12) <u>is</u> destructive, but rituals can be fun: birthday parties, holiday tradition, running to meet (13) <u>Dad. When</u> he's home from work. In most cases, they repeat again and again joyous moments which can be anticipated, counted on, and (14) <u>remembering</u>.

Activities which include work not only are necessities of our lives, but also are rewarding in and of (15) <u>itself.</u> They allow for (16) <u>mastery</u>, excellence, craftsmanship, and the expression of a great variety of skills and talents. However, if there is discomfort in a (17) <u>relationship going on between two people</u> when these activities (modes of structuring time) cease, it is safe to say (18) <u>they're</u> is little intimacy. Some

11. A. NO CHANGE
    B. and are games
    C. and are also games
    D. and are some diverse games

12. A. NO CHANGE
    B. are
    C. isn't
    D. was

13. A. NO CHANGE
    B. Dad; when
    C. Dad when
    D. Dad, when

14. A. NO CHANGE
    B. were remembered
    C. having been remembered
    D. remembered

15. A. NO CHANGE
    B. themselves
    C. ourselves
    D. it

16. A. NO CHANGE
    B. a master
    C. masters
    D. mastering

17. A. NO CHANGE
    B. ongoing on relationship between two different people
    C. relationship in and between two people
    D. relationship between two people

18. A. NO CHANGE
    B. their
    C. there
    D. they

(19) <u>couple's</u> program their entire time together with frantic activity. The activity itself was not destructive unless the compulsion to keep busy is (20) <u>one, and</u> the same as the compulsion to keep away from your partner.

-Harris, p. 153

19. A. NO CHANGE
    B. couples
    C. couples'
    D. coupled

20. A. NO CHANGE
    B. one; and
    C. one: and
    D. one and

Arthur and Pulley

After work one day I set out for the (21) ballpark, I wanted to catch a Tokyo Giants game. (22) I marched out to the bleachers only to find them completely full. It was standing room only six deep in fans. (23) Discouraging, I turned back, hoping food would help. (24) Pass up the hot dog (25) kiosks; I bought a roasted squid on a stick.

The Tokyo Giants were playing the Hiroshima Carp. The players (26) to each other bowed; the game was about to begin. I glanced up at the electronic scoreboard that displayed (in Chinese characters) all the (27) players names and a vast array of information, including wind direction and speed.

In point of fact, the Tokyo Giants, it had been explained to me, were actually the Yomiuri Giants. Actual names were not taken from their

21. A. NO CHANGE
    B. ballpark; I
    C. ballpark–I
    D. ballpark I

22. A. NO CHANGE
    B. I, marching out to the bleachers
    C. To the bleachers I marched out
    D. To the bleachers out I marched

23. A. NO CHANGE
    B. Discourages
    C. Discouraged
    D. Having discouraged

24. A. NO CHANGE
    B. Passed
    C. Passes
    D. Passing

25. A. NO CHANGE
    B. kiosks, I
    C. kiosks - I
    D. kiosks I

26. A. NO CHANGE
    B. to each they bowed
    C. bowed to each other
    D. one to the other bowed

27. A. NO CHANGE
    B. players'
    C. player's
    D. player

geographic headquarters but rather from the companies that owned them, such as the Yomiuri news firm that owned the Giants, or the Hanshin railway company (28) who were the owners of the Hanshin Tigers. But what in the world, I wondered, were the Nippon Ham Fighters?

The noise surged as the game began, with cheerleaders prancing atop the dugout roofs, exhorting their teams, (29) they flailed the air with pompoms and banners in the teams' colors, and beating an ancient native drum. The noise level and the sections of "home" and "away" rooters reminded me more of American college football than baseball. Horns blared, people howled, toilet paper and confetti streamers arched through the night sky.

Several differences from

28. A. NO CHANGE
    B. that had ownership of the Hanshin Tigers
    C. who the ownership of the Hanshin Tigers belonged to
    D. that owned the Hanshin Tigers

29. A. NO CHANGE
    B. they would flail
    C. flailing
    D. they were flailing

American baseball practices were glaring: every time a foul or a home run carried the ball into the riotous stands, it was (30) politely returned to the field. Propriety prevailed, even amidst hysteria. Also, no matter how obvious, the official scorers virtually refused to charge fielders with errors.

-Katzenstein, pp. 28-30

30. A. NO CHANGE
    B. insert after "to"
    C. insert after "field"
    D. insert before "it"

Most school psychologists and counselors feel that the family is the most significant, single influence on the development of the child. The family is the primary structure that provides the developing human being with (31) my attitudes, beliefs, values, sense of self, and (32) provides related behaviors. Educational researchers (33) have showed that academic performance, persistence, and self-concept are strongly related to family background variables and interactions.

The school system is probably the second most important (34) structure of the environments that influences the developing human (35) being when a student is having difficulty adapting to the school system (as manifested by poor grades, truancy, acting out, (36) school phobias, or vandalism), the school system's intervention plans have,

31. A. NO CHANGE
    B. their
    C. his or her
    D. your

32. A. NO CHANGE
    B. providing related behaviors
    C. then provided related behaviors
    D. related behaviors

33. A. NO CHANGE
    B. have shown
    C. having been showing
    D. showing

34. A. NO CHANGE
    B. structural environment
    C. structure's environment
    D. environmental structure

35. A. NO CHANGE
    B. being. When
    C. being, when
    D. being: when

36. A. NO CHANGE
    B. and also school
    C. plus school
    D. and school

for the most part, tried to influence the individual student in isolation from the most significant influence in the (37) childrens' life—the family.

    From the family-systems perspective, many of these intervention programs (such as punishments and individual or group counseling) are doomed to failure. This is true if the family's influence and (38) valued system are different from the school system's intended behavior change. (39) For example, the school may try to stop a student from fighting at school, while the parent's message to the child is, "Don't let anyone push you around. Stand up for yourself." From the family-systems perspective, it is imperative that the family (40) be involved. If you wish to see more effective and enduring behavioral changes at school.

    - Valentine, p. 15-16

37. A. NO CHANGE
    B. childs'
    C. children's
    D. child's

38. A. NO CHANGE
    B. valuable
    C. value
    D. valuing

39. A. NO CHANGE
    B. On the other hand
    C. Next
    D. Previously

40. A. NO CHANGE
    B. involved if
    C. involved; if
    D. Involved, if

Name_____ Date_____ Score_____

PRACTICE EXIT EXAM TEN

Punishment can inhibit a child's (1) behavior many psychologists believe physical punishment, such as spanking or (2) hits should not be used at all. Physical punishment modifies the behavior of the child in the short (3) run but its use is also (4) associated with many negative outcomes.

The first and (5) most effective serious punishment is an increase in aggression, especially among boys. For example, parents who used punishment and threats had more aggressive sons than those who did not use such techniques. (6) Last, parents who use physical punishment may serve as models of aggressiveness for (7) your children. Third, children may learn that violence is an acceptable method for

1. A. NO CHANGE
   B. behavior – many
   C. behavior, many
   D. behavior. Many

2. A. NO CHANGE
   B. hitting
   C. hit
   D. having hit

3. A. NO CHANGE
   B. run. But
   C. run, but
   D. run–but

4. A. NO CHANGE
   B. having associates
   C. associating
   D. associates

5. A. NO CHANGE
   B. most serious effect of punishment
   C. seriously effect of mostly punishment
   D. punishment of serious effect

6. A. NO CHANGE
   B. As mentioned above
   C. Second
   D. Previously

7. A. NO CHANGE
   B. his
   C. our
   D. their

resolving conflicts rather (8) <u>then</u> other methods. (9) <u>Conversely</u>, children who are punished frequently avoid the person (10) <u>that</u> does the punishing.

-Kestner, p. 298

8. A. NO CHANGE
   B. than
   C. that
   D. omit underlined portion

9. A. NO CHANGE
   B. Last
   C. Similarly
   D. Thus

10. A. NO CHANGE
    B. which
    C. who
    D. whose

There are some very real differences between fathers and mothers in terms of their involvement with the child. In general, research shows that compared to mothers, fathers spend (11) comparatively less time with children. This may not be because fathers work outside of the (12) home even when both parents are home, fathers generally spend less time with children than mothers. In 1983 Pleck reported that (13) employers of fatherless children less than five years old spend an average of 27 minutes (14) once per every day in caregiving or other activities with their children. Even when a mother works outside of the home, fathers only spend about one-third the time that (15) mothers spend in parenting activities. Why the disparity? One reason for the lack of involvement by fathers may be due to resistance by

11. A. NO CHANGE
    B. insert after "father"
    C. insert after "children
    D. insert after "less"

12. A. NO CHANGE
    B. home. Even
    C. home (even
    D. home—even

13. A. NO CHANGE
    B. employment of fathers with children
    C. fathers of employed children
    D. employed fathers with children

14. A. NO CHANGE
    B. a day
    C. once
    D. each per day

15. A. NO CHANGE
    B. she
    C. they
    D. themselves

the mothers! Only 23 percent of employed mothers and 31 percent of unemployed (16) mothers. Stated that they wanted more help from (17) them. (18) In this particular study, it (19) might conclude that the (20) motherings were reluctant to share their role with the fathers.

-Kestner, p. 298

16. A. NO CHANGE
    B. mothers; stated
    C. mothers stating
    D. mothers stated

17. A. NO CHANGE
    B. themselves
    C. fathers
    D. mothers

18. A. NO CHANGE
    B. In a study particular to this
    C. In a study, particularly, this
    D. In studying particular to this

19. A. NO CHANGE
    B. might be concluded
    C. having been concluded
    D. has been concluding

20. A. NO CHANGE
    B. mother's
    C. mothers'
    D. mothers

If there is any truth to the idea that castles can be haunted, then Chillingham should certainly afford shelter to many ghosts of its departed (21) <u>owners, and</u> former dwellers. In this land of ancient dwellings, (22) <u>continuously</u> very few houses have been lived in from so early a date. For almost eight hundred years, the long procession (23) <u>stretches. A procession of</u> people who have lived, (24) <u>and loved</u> and suffered therein.

Chillingham Castle is full of romance, and in times of old, the castle (being so close to the Borderland) was the scene of many a raid from its Scottish neighbors. (25) <u>Its</u> dungeons were probably seldom (26) <u>without some inmate unfortunately</u> who had been captured. One can still see today

21. A. NO CHANGE
    B. owners; and
    C. owners and
    D. owners—and

22. A. NO CHANGE
    B. insert after "in"
    C. insert after "few"
    C. insert after "so"

23. A. NO CHANGE
    B. stretches (of
    C. stretches: of
    D. stretches; of

24. A. NO CHANGE
    B. loving,
    C. and also loved
    D. loved,

25. A. NO CHANGE
    B. It's
    C. Its'
    D. It is

26. A. NO CHANGE
    B. unfortunately without an inmate
    C. without some unfortunate inmate
    D. some inmate unfortunately without

GO ON TO THE NEXT PAGE

Arthur and Pulley

ancient initials and scratchings of those who passed the time by counting the number of days of their weary imprisonment.

    One of the best known and authenticated ghosts of the castle (27) <u>are</u> that of Lady Mary Berkeley, wife of Lord Grey. She is still looking for her errant (28) <u>husband that</u> gentleman ran away with her own sister, Lady Henrietta, (29) <u>finally</u> giving rise to a great scandal. A lawsuit ensued. All of this occurred during the reign of Charles II. The end of it all was a heartless desertion. The poor lady was left in her dark and lonely castle with only a fatherless baby girl as her companion. To this day, the rustle of her (30) <u>threads</u> is sometimes heard along the corridors and stairs. As the disappointed and anxious ghost passes by, a chill, as of cold air, seems to sweep through the dank halls.   -Chillingham

27. A. NO CHANGE
    B. to be
    C. were
    D. is

28. A. NO CHANGE
    B. husband. That
    C. husband, that
    D. husband–that

29. A. NO CHANGE
    B. because
    C. thus
    D. however

30. A. NO CHANGE
    B. rags
    C. attire
    D. dress

Arthur and Pulley

How long had she (31) laid there? How many weeks, (32) and also how many days had she been unaware of her surroundings. She did not know, nor did she care enough to ask. Earlier this evening after (33) vespers. The nun who sat by her bed had suddenly gasped and run to fetch the (34) board, and stick. She (35) had heard her race through the cloister, furiously beating the death board.

    Somehow she had lived through sixty-three summers, playing her tedious roles in the convent, forever smiling, never (36) allowed the world to glimpse the real woman. Quickly, she corrected (37) her. To him she had sometimes revealed her true (38) self, but even he could not accept her. The letters, those shameless shreds, those offerings of truth delivered up to his aghast silence; her hands clutched the coverlet

31. A. NO CHANGE
    B. lay
    C. lain
    D. lying

32. A. NO CHANGE
    B. or how many days
    C. and the days, how many
    D. or the days, also how many

33. A. NO CHANGE
    B. vespers the
    C. vespers; the
    D. vespers, the

34. A. NO CHANGE
    B. board and stick
    C. board, stick
    D. board; and stick

35. A. NO CHANGE
    B. had been hearing
    C. had been heard
    D. hearing

36. A. NO CHANGE
    B. being allowed
    C. allowing
    D. have allowed

37. A. NO CHANGE
    B. it
    C. him
    D. herself

38. A. NO CHANGE
    B. self; but
    C. self. But
    D. self but

in (39) memory which stings. Ah, my very sweet friend, she thought, you didn't understand my (40) love in the end you learned to love God, and even, in your own way, to love me.   It had taken so long.

-Meade, pp. 9; 11

39. A. NO CHANGE
    B. the memory, stinging
    C. stinging memory
    D. stinging of the memory

40. A. NO CHANGE
    B. love—in
    C. love...in
    D. love. In

SCANTRONS FOR PRACTICE EXIT EXAMS

Practice Exit Exam One

Practice Exit Exam Two

1. Ⓐ Ⓑ Ⓒ Ⓓ Ⓔ
2. Ⓐ Ⓑ Ⓒ Ⓓ Ⓔ
3. Ⓐ Ⓑ Ⓒ Ⓓ Ⓔ
4. Ⓐ Ⓑ Ⓒ Ⓓ Ⓔ
5. Ⓐ Ⓑ Ⓒ Ⓓ Ⓔ
6. Ⓐ Ⓑ Ⓒ Ⓓ Ⓔ
7. Ⓐ Ⓑ Ⓒ Ⓓ Ⓔ
8. Ⓐ Ⓑ Ⓒ Ⓓ Ⓔ
9. Ⓐ Ⓑ Ⓒ Ⓓ Ⓔ
10. Ⓐ Ⓑ Ⓒ Ⓓ Ⓔ
11. Ⓐ Ⓑ Ⓒ Ⓓ Ⓔ
12. Ⓐ Ⓑ Ⓒ Ⓓ Ⓔ
13. Ⓐ Ⓑ Ⓒ Ⓓ Ⓔ
14. Ⓐ Ⓑ Ⓒ Ⓓ Ⓔ
15. Ⓐ Ⓑ Ⓒ Ⓓ Ⓔ
16. Ⓐ Ⓑ Ⓒ Ⓓ Ⓔ
17. Ⓐ Ⓑ Ⓒ Ⓓ Ⓔ
18. Ⓐ Ⓑ Ⓒ Ⓓ Ⓔ
19. Ⓐ Ⓑ Ⓒ Ⓓ Ⓔ
20. Ⓐ Ⓑ Ⓒ Ⓓ Ⓔ
21. Ⓐ Ⓑ Ⓒ Ⓓ Ⓔ
22. Ⓐ Ⓑ Ⓒ Ⓓ Ⓔ
23. Ⓐ Ⓑ Ⓒ Ⓓ Ⓔ
24. Ⓐ Ⓑ Ⓒ Ⓓ Ⓔ
25. Ⓐ Ⓑ Ⓒ Ⓓ Ⓔ
26. Ⓐ Ⓑ Ⓒ Ⓓ Ⓔ
27. Ⓐ Ⓑ Ⓒ Ⓓ Ⓔ
28. Ⓐ Ⓑ Ⓒ Ⓓ Ⓔ
29. Ⓐ Ⓑ Ⓒ Ⓓ Ⓔ
30. Ⓐ Ⓑ Ⓒ Ⓓ Ⓔ
31. Ⓐ Ⓑ Ⓒ Ⓓ Ⓔ
32. Ⓐ Ⓑ Ⓒ Ⓓ Ⓔ
33. Ⓐ Ⓑ Ⓒ Ⓓ Ⓔ
34. Ⓐ Ⓑ Ⓒ Ⓓ Ⓔ
35. Ⓐ Ⓑ Ⓒ Ⓓ Ⓔ
36. Ⓐ Ⓑ Ⓒ Ⓓ Ⓔ
37. Ⓐ Ⓑ Ⓒ Ⓓ Ⓔ
38. Ⓐ Ⓑ Ⓒ Ⓓ Ⓔ
39. Ⓐ Ⓑ Ⓒ Ⓓ Ⓔ
40. Ⓐ Ⓑ Ⓒ Ⓓ Ⓔ

INSTRUCTIONS

* Use a No. 2 pencil.
* Fill circles completely.
* Erase cleanly.

Practice Exit Exam Three

Practice Exit Exam Four

Practice Exit Exam Five

Practice Exit Exam Six

Practice Exit Exam Seven

Practice Exit Exam Eight

INSTRUCTIONS

* Use a No. 2 pencil.
* Fill circles completely.
* Erase cleanly.

1. Ⓐ Ⓑ Ⓒ Ⓓ Ⓔ
2. Ⓐ Ⓑ Ⓒ Ⓓ Ⓔ
3. Ⓐ Ⓑ Ⓒ Ⓓ Ⓔ
4. Ⓐ Ⓑ Ⓒ Ⓓ Ⓔ
5. Ⓐ Ⓑ Ⓒ Ⓓ Ⓔ
6. Ⓐ Ⓑ Ⓒ Ⓓ Ⓔ
7. Ⓐ Ⓑ Ⓒ Ⓓ Ⓔ
8. Ⓐ Ⓑ Ⓒ Ⓓ Ⓔ
9. Ⓐ Ⓑ Ⓒ Ⓓ Ⓔ
10. Ⓐ Ⓑ Ⓒ Ⓓ Ⓔ
11. Ⓐ Ⓑ Ⓒ Ⓓ Ⓔ
12. Ⓐ Ⓑ Ⓒ Ⓓ Ⓔ
13. Ⓐ Ⓑ Ⓒ Ⓓ Ⓔ
14. Ⓐ Ⓑ Ⓒ Ⓓ Ⓔ
15. Ⓐ Ⓑ Ⓒ Ⓓ Ⓔ
16. Ⓐ Ⓑ Ⓒ Ⓓ Ⓔ
17. Ⓐ Ⓑ Ⓒ Ⓓ Ⓔ
18. Ⓐ Ⓑ Ⓒ Ⓓ Ⓔ
19. Ⓐ Ⓑ Ⓒ Ⓓ Ⓔ
20. Ⓐ Ⓑ Ⓒ Ⓓ Ⓔ
21. Ⓐ Ⓑ Ⓒ Ⓓ Ⓔ
22. Ⓐ Ⓑ Ⓒ Ⓓ Ⓔ
23. Ⓐ Ⓑ Ⓒ Ⓓ Ⓔ
24. Ⓐ Ⓑ Ⓒ Ⓓ Ⓔ
25. Ⓐ Ⓑ Ⓒ Ⓓ Ⓔ
26. Ⓐ Ⓑ Ⓒ Ⓓ Ⓔ
27. Ⓐ Ⓑ Ⓒ Ⓓ Ⓔ
28. Ⓐ Ⓑ Ⓒ Ⓓ Ⓔ
29. Ⓐ Ⓑ Ⓒ Ⓓ Ⓔ
30. Ⓐ Ⓑ Ⓒ Ⓓ Ⓔ
31. Ⓐ Ⓑ Ⓒ Ⓓ Ⓔ
32. Ⓐ Ⓑ Ⓒ Ⓓ Ⓔ
33. Ⓐ Ⓑ Ⓒ Ⓓ Ⓔ
34. Ⓐ Ⓑ Ⓒ Ⓓ Ⓔ
35. Ⓐ Ⓑ Ⓒ Ⓓ Ⓔ
36. Ⓐ Ⓑ Ⓒ Ⓓ Ⓔ
37. Ⓐ Ⓑ Ⓒ Ⓓ Ⓔ
38. Ⓐ Ⓑ Ⓒ Ⓓ Ⓔ
39. Ⓐ Ⓑ Ⓒ Ⓓ Ⓔ
40. Ⓐ Ⓑ Ⓒ Ⓓ Ⓔ

Practice Exit Exam Nine

Practice Exit Exam Ten

CHAPTER SIX: WRITING THE EXIT ESSAY

The first order of business when writing your exit essay is getting control of yourself. You, the student, are faced with a blank page, and your assignment is to write an essay. A red flag should *not* go up immediately. Your temperature should not rise. You should not become faint because the exercise of formal written expression is one of the many means by which each human communicates. The ability to transmit feelings and thoughts is innate and can be cultivated in each of us to achieve various levels of proficiency. Getting control of yourself means making your enormous repository of prior knowledge work to your advantage when given writing assignments.

As children, we master *receptive language* first and *expressive language* second; most of us are introduced to and begin to learn both by three years of age. *Receptive language* is understanding what is said or what is read to you. *Expressive language* is writing or speaking. Oftentimes to help students gain confidence and earnestly work toward writing well, we tell them to "talk" to us on paper. We ask them to consider how many years of experience they have had talking. "All my life" is the answer they usually give. We stress this point because we want them to understand that they have experience with language that they can bring to their writing.

Though most students rarely remember how or when they learned to speak, psychologists' research indicates that human language development is rapid. More specifically, a baby's "babbling" at six months, the earliest speech that infants produce, contains all sounds of human speech. And by the age of three years, a child has a vocabulary of about 1000 words(*Essentials of Psychology 261*). So, yes, your answer can also be "all of my life." A second comment from students is "just let me tell you;

I can say it much clearer than I can write it."

With speaking, many of us feel free, not "rule bound." Many aspects of conversational English make it more enjoyable than writing. First during conversation, our listener rarely interjects critical remarks like "I didn't hear your subject and verb agree. I heard a misplaced modifier. You are missing a parenthetical. Your comments are not organized well." Instead, the content of what you are saying (i.e., the scoop, the story, the venting, the plea along with gestures) engages the listener. Second, the non-verbal signals or body language assists in clarifying the point. Next, your voice is animated, using pitch and range to emphasize the highlights and important parts. Finally, in most cases our audience is interested in what you have to say.

Consequently, we are more practiced, more confident, and more comfortable with speaking and sometimes afraid to attempt transferring this type of expressive language (speaking) to the second type of language, writing. Students should feel just as confident with putting thoughts on the page because like talking, students have a similar, long, familiar background with the written word. For many, "being read to" began the process. The first durable plastic book (of pictures) you teethed on may have been your earliest encounter. Also, parents or siblings read to you, or perhaps you interacted with popular toy characters with read-a-long tapes and books.

By preschool, you could probably write your name. In kindergarten, you learned initial reading and writing skills. At five years of age, you wrote (or had someone write for you) three-sentence stories (beginning, middle, and end) such as these examples illustrate:

I went to my grandma's house. I swam. I saw yummy black berrys and beautiful birds. I herd a bird. I smelled roses. I felt happy. (Kindergartener)

I went to Six Flags over Georgia. I rode the Robin ride. I saw Batman's car. I heard that I was going to see Batman. I smelled a Batman sticker. I felt great when I got back home. (Kindergartener)

At eight or nine years old, you could write more detail, and the essay length expanded to seven sentences. At this third grade level, you could describe your new puppy's coloring, his habits, and his maintenance.

Bobo is my brown Labrador retriever who is very playful. He runs and jumps to catch the ball and the frisbee that I throw to him. I have even taught him some tricks. He gets his walking leash and brings it to me everyday, even though it is not time for his walk. My mother hates it when Bobo knocks over the trash can and digs through it. Sometimes she makes me clean up the mess he made, but she has to clean up most of the time. I tell her not to get mad because he is just a puppy.

As you progress through grade levels, the same story becomes more complex.

The essay develops more fully into a two-page product. The beginning, middle, and end consists of four or more paragraphs, has more enhanced detail, and is more cohesive. The essay also has advanced vocabulary and a varied and complex sentence structure.

Fishing is not a pleasant memory for me. I was about ten years old when I went on my first and last fishing trip. It started out as an adventurous outing to Ruby Lake but the trip soon turned into a painful event that ended the fun for that day and ruined any chance of my attempting to fish again....

Since only my aunt (the instructor) and my sister had caught a fish, my cousins and I were instructed to move to the other side of the pond to try our luck. During this process is when I decided that never again would I go fishing. One of my cousins was walking in front of me, and I noticed something shiny under his shoe. I told him to stop and let me take a look at it. To our surprise, a triple fish hook lure was stuck in the bottom of his shoe. So, I took it upon myself to take it out, determining that the hook would work itself into his foot. My aunt said to be careful, but I thought I knew what I was doing. Somehow in that one second the hook came out of his shoe, the hook stuck in my thumb the same time. I am sure my frantic screaming could be heard a mile from that lake... After the twenty minutes it took to strategically remove the lure that was entangled in my nerves, we were all ready to go home.

It has been quite a few years since that tragic event occurred. In brief, I do not like fishing, and to this day I have the scar to prove it.

(Althea, 15 years old)

Another important skill that you developed over time is your years of reading other writers. Reading other writings has helped to train you as a writer. From reading about history, art, music, geography, science, and literature (fiction and non-fiction), your background knowledge expanded. These models helped you recognize organization, cohesion, support, tone, and style. Consequently, you developed a schemata. Brenda Smith (2002) defines schema (plural *schemata*) as "the skeleton of knowledge in your mind on a particular subject. As you expand your knowledge, the skeleton grows" (*Breaking Through 34*). That is, the skeleton is fleshed out as you acquire more information on the subject. For instance, elementary subject matter is foundation for more complex materials in the higher grades. In second-grade mathematics students learn addition and subtraction. In ninth grade, students learn to add and subtract variables in algebraic formulas. Another instance is learning in the third grade that Abraham Lincoln was the sixteenth president. In sixth grade students learn about the Civil War. In college history teachers assume the students know the two previous facts and begin to enhance discussions surrounding Lincoln's tactics during the Civil War. Like the math and history teacher, college English teachers know that students have read novels and short stories, have written developed paragraphs, and have explored creative writing. English teachers know that from infancy, you have had experience with language.

In addition to you, yourself, building schemata, all of your teachers have worked to help you strengthen your skills. This has allowed you freedom to experiment with various writing styles, aiding you in building an enormous word bank, and encouraging you to generate limitless ideas. With these tools that you already have when you enter the college classroom, you will captivate your audience.

Jumpstarting an outline is the most important part of the pre-writing process. How do you end up with a final product/essay, one that you can feel confident about, that you feel good about handing into your professor? Obviously, you must go through a process; you can't just start writing until you finish four or five pages and think that such a paper will be acceptable. Writing an essay takes forethought. Your teacher can tell if you have spent time thinking about the topic and organizing your thoughts so that they come out in a clear and coherent manner. The process takes some time and effort, but your grades will improve if you think before you write.

This preliminary stage includes drawing from your prior knowledge on the topic. It also includes completing some research to find out more about the topic. Depending on the writing assignment, research may range from simply talking to your peers to conducting a formal search of twenty sources. A second part of this preliminary stage is designing a layout or "roughing out" a framework. This brainstorming is a liberating exercise that allows you to explore thoroughly a topic, an idea, or an argument. You can practice a pre-writing strategy to match your learning style, and then adopt that strategy if it works for you. Though people are not usually one type of learner exclusively, read the descriptions below to determine your primary learning style (these are the most often recognized categories).

Visual learners: You rely upon "seeing" the topic, idea, or argument. Outlining your ideas provides immediate structure and order. You are able to visualize "general from specific" and "topic from supporting detail." This technique helps you shape and organize as you generate concepts. Other methods are mapping, graphing, or charting.

Auditory learners: You do well when you "hear" the topic, idea, or argument. Buying or renting tapes on the topic is a strategy which may prove beneficial to an auditory learner. Listening to others in discussion groups, having a study buddy read to you, or reading your written notes aloud gives you the opportunity to sound out your assumptions. Reading to others in small groups or to a partner helps you clarify the points you are making because you receive immediate feedback.

Kinesthetic learners: You like to try things out–a type of "hands on" approach to learning. You enjoy movement. For your topic, idea, or argument to come to life, you must go and experience it in the present or retrace prior events. After this experiential learning process, you can draft a description; it may seem like your thoughts are incomplete or running together, but that is fine. You will be able to find a thread of an idea to develop into a cohesive essay.

Written expressive: You work better with pen and paper in hand. You feel best when you freewrite in an automatic stream-of-consciousness mode. You like journal writing because you respond easily to experiences you encounter through activities such as diary and letter writing. Jotting down your thoughts "in the moment" clarifies your clear central idea and specific details.

> You can utilize this pre-writing strategy when you become anxious about writing for your professor. It includes drawing upon concrete strategies to aid you in the beginning stages.

After the announcement of the assignment, your mind begins to search its database for prior knowledge of the subject; it begins to turn over question after question. This thought process is one of the best ways to begin an assignment. To help you put pen to paper, practice the suggested process to "jumpstart" an outline for the essay. Read through the method below to visualize how this process can aid you in organizing an outline and writing an essay.

PROCESS JUMPSTART

The first directive is to proceed as if you were a *crime-scene investigator*. This strategy will help you organize your thinking before you begin the writing assignment. Like a crime scene investigator, you analyze the situation from as many angles as possible. Let's briefly examine the steps by which an investigator proceeds.

Step I

The investigator looks over the entire scene to gain control of the situation, to educate himself/herself, and to become aware of all circumstances that may influence any final decisions. The first step involves asking initial questions.

Step II

The investigator then thinks about the scene. At this stage, he/she is organizing the evidence into contributing causes. Also he/she is reasoning by using analytical skills (i.e., deductive or inductive reasoning, depending on his or her personal style of thinking). *Inductive reasoning* is moving from specific, detailed information to a general thesis. That is, the investigator looks at specific clues and comes up with a general theory of what happened. *Deductive reasoning* is thinking of a general thesis, then finding specific, detailed information to support that thesis. That is, the investigator has a general idea about what happened; then, s/he looks for clues to prove it. As a writer, you will choose which type of reasoning (inductive or deductive) works for you for each particular essay you are asked to write.

Step III

Next the investigator links the present information with prior knowledge (i.e., schemata). By studying the database of clues and information gathered, previous similar incidences, numerous texts or cases read, or other police experiences may be recalled. This is the step which establishes an information base. The investigator can formulate clear-cut decisions later by organizing and identifying patterns within the newly-formed database.

Step IV

At this step, the investigator can formally outline the information to gain a visual representation of the crime. This step is essential to writing his report.

Step V

Finally, he must write the report.

When we apply the same steps to writing, we get the same results. Let's give this method a try.

USING PROCESS JUMPSTART

The assigned topic is

WAYS IN WHICH WOMEN ATTRACT UNWANTED ATTENTION FROM MEN

"Jumpstart" an outline for this topic by using Process Jumpstart before you even write one word!

Step I: Ask initial questions.

- ❏ Have I had this experience or do I know someone who has?
- ❏ Have I seen a situation comedy, drama, soap, or movie that has this issue in the plot?
- ❏ Have I read an article that focuses on this topic?
- ❏ What age group of women should I consider?
- ❏ What are the types of unwanted attention?
- ❏ Do the way in which women act attract unwanted attention?
- ❏ Can I already give examples of women attracting unwanted attention from men?

List other questions you can think of:

_____

_____

_____

(Note: After listing your questions, other ideas may come to you that your instructor may not have explicitly addressed in class. Don't hesitate to discuss any "new" ideas you have with him or her.)

Step II: Organize the evidence and information by jotting down notes.

As mentioned in the previous discussion on Step II (page 211), two types of reasoning were presented: deductive and inductive reasoning. For this example, we will use inductive reasoning. Therefore, you will begin by listing your "clues" that suggest that women attract unwanted attention from men.

Inductive: Listing of examples of women's behavior which may attract unwanted attention (from actual college student essays)

- Ways Women Dress
    - women dress in short dresses
    - women dress in form-fitting dresses
    - women wear short shorts
    - women wear cropped tops
- Ways Women Behave
    - women flirt with men
    - women get intoxicated at parties
    - women (in small groups) pretend not to check men out, but they do

Can you add to this list?

_____

_____

_____

Although you can probably say that the portrayal of women aged 18 to 24 in the media shows attractive women dressed in the latest fashions, it's a good idea to sit down and again view women on TV, in magazines, and perhaps at parties and on campus. Yes, they may be wearing form-fitting dresses, tops, pants or short skirts or short shorts. And yes, most wear makeup–medium to heavy–and look like they have stepped off the model's catwalk. But by viewing the media again and observing women at parties, you will gather evidence for your essay, and *this evidence, along with your previous experience, will provide the main support for your essay.*

Important note: if the evidence does NOT support your thesis, you will need to change your thesis!

Inductive: Listing of examples of unwanted attention from men

- Ways Some Men Respond to Signals (and respond with unwanted attention)
    - heckling women by whistling, name calling, making gestures
    - persistently asking women for their phone numbers
    - giving women gifts (no encouragement from the women)

| Arthur and Pate | Page 215 |

- dropping notes in girls' backpacks in class
- following or stalking women

Add to this list:
_____
_____
_____

Step III: **Link present information with prior knowledge.**

External Experiences:
In many movies, women wear tight, short skirts and cropped tops. Even when handing a client a cup of coffee, their body language is suggestive.

External experiences you've observed:
_____
_____
_____

Previous Personal Experiences:
In high school during my senior year, a group of popular girls used to wear the tightest clothes (especially sweaters), and all the guys used to stare at them when they walked by. The boys would hoot and whistle, beg for dates or phone numbers. The girls would bat their overly made-up eyelashes and innocently say, "Do you mean me?" Some of them would just keep walking, "ignoring" the whistles.

Your previous personal experiences:
_____
_____
_____

Present Personal Experience:

On my way to class, I saw a girl get out of her car, and she was trying to stack six or eight books and notebooks in her arms. She kept dropping two or three books every step she took. She was wearing some incredibly tight jeans and a tube top. She bent over to pick up the books! (She didn't merely stoop down to get them!) Two guys saw her and literally ran across the street to help her with the books.

At the club the other night, two girls made a bet to see who could drink their beer the fastest. They were tied at three beers apiece, and the next beer was supposed to declare the winner. Neither of them won because each spent the rest of the evening in the bathroom!

Your present personal experience:

_____

_____

_____

Step IV. Now it is time to look back over the steps that you have worked through to take stock or inventory to make sure that all the pieces of evidence created so far are related to the topic that you have been assigned. So at this stage, let's review the information that we have generated.

In Step I, we merely listed questions related to our topic. In Step II, however, we began listing evidence to support the topic. The ability to start outlining begins with Step II. But how do we fit the information and support into an outline format? Let's methodically look at each bit of information we gathered:

First, we came up with three concepts related to the topic:

I. Ways Women Dress

II. Ways Women Behave

III. Ways Men Respond to Signals from Women

This outline is too skimpy. We need to flesh it out more. Continuing to look at what we brainstormed in Step II, we can see that we determined *how* women dress, *how* women behave, and *how* men respond to signals from women. Let's write these underneath the appropriate category.

II. Ways Women Behave
   A. Flirting
      1. In general:
      2. At parties:

III. Ways Men Respond to Signals from Women
   A. Heckling and harassing

Next, in our brainstorming session, we thought of *examples* of choice of clothing, flirting, and heckling and harassing. So we can flesh out our outline even more with these examples.

I. Ways Women Dress
   A. Choice of clothing
      1. Short dresses, form-fitting clothing

You look back and fill in the examples for II and III

II. Ways Women Behave
   A. Flirting
      1.

III. Ways Men Respond to Signals from Women
   A. Heckling and harassing
      1.

Last, we thought of *anecdotes as examples*. So, we add these to the outline to make it complete. The first one is done for you. You complete II and III.

I. Ways Women Dress
   A. Choice of clothing
      1. Short dresses, form-fitting clothing
      2. In high school during my senior year, a group of popular girls used to wear the tightest clothes (especially sweaters)
      3. On my way to class, I saw a girl get out of her car. She was trying to stack six or eight books and notebooks in her arms. The girl was wearing some incredibly tight jeans and a tube top.

II. Ways Women Behave
   A. Flirting
      1. In general:
      2. At parties

III. Ways Men Respond to Signals from Women
   A. Heckling and harassing
      1.
      2.

Taking time to work through a pre-writing exercise and writing an outline will save you much grief. You may be doubting your ability to write a good essay because you have convinced yourself that you hate writing. Or you may not have had much experience writing essays at your previous school. To help rid yourself of all these doubts and fears, you need to practice one or more of the pre-writing strategies.

Now that we have done the pre-writing work for the topic, *WAYS IN WHICH WOMEN ATTRACT UNWANTED ATTENTION FROM MEN*, let's begin writing the essay itself which is *Step V*.

FLASH: Many times students will still have trouble writing on that blank page. Don't forget that many resources already exist, and they will help you get past that moment of anxiety. Some of these ready-made starters are newspaper or magazine headlines about recent controversial issues. You may have watched a news broadcast or television documentary that explains the background about an assigned topic. Reading anecdotes, conducting a survey, or interviewing an interesting person can elicit ideas or help you crystalize an hypothesis.

Step V: Write the essay. Use your pre-thinking skills and previous experiences to organize and support your thesis.

You now have narrowed your topic, have written a plan or outline, and have sat down to actually write. The objective at this point is to get all your thoughts onto the page by building your essay step-by-step. An essay is composed of three basic aspects: the introduction, the body paragraph (or paragraphs), and the conclusion. You will begin by writing the introduction. This step in the process will take you to a good but rough draft.

WRITING THE INTRODUCTION

Believe it or not, there is a formula or technique for writing an introduction, and it works. There are two parts involved. We will call them Part A, the hook, and Part B, the thesis. Please refer to the formula below.

Formula for Writing the Introduction

Introduction = Part A + Part B

OR

Introduction = Hook + Thesis

Part A = The Hook

At this stage of the plan, you want to gain the readers' attention by offering something unique, something they haven't come across before in their reading. Suppose you were in the line at the grocery store and the title of a news story caught your eye: "Rock Star Involved in Money-Laundering Scandal." Even though you know it could just be hype, you will find yourself scanning the article to find out which rock star had been arrested. When you realize it's someone you have admired, you continue to read. Suddenly you realize the cashier is waiting for you to pay. (By the way, you're hooked now and must buy the magazine.) To achieve the same response from the reader when you write, you also need to come up with a *hook*.

Remember your topic is *WAYS IN WHICH WOMEN ATTRACT UNWANTED ATTENTION FROM MEN*, so how are you going to interest your readers? Here are some suggestions:

1. *Try a headline* - go to a recent newspaper or news magazine and grab a title which will captivate the readers' interest immediately: "Suitable or Seductive"

2. *Select a sentence or two* from an article that is related to your topic:
"My guy friend puts his arm around me a lot. Does this mean I have given him signals?"

3. *Write an anecdote or short account* that illustrates your topic. An anecdote can be a personal experience or an account based on something you have heard about from a boy/girlfriend, a relative, a close friend, or a news reporter. For example,

My girlfriend gave me her opinion the other day: "When a guy is attracted to you, he might nonchalantly toss his arm around you, pretending he is reaching for a can of soda on the other side of your shoulder. If you let his arm linger there a second longer than necessary, then you are giving him the go-ahead signal. After all, he's just a friend, right?"

Personal Experience

On my way to class, I saw a girl get out of her car. She was trying to stack six or eight books and notebooks in her arms and she kept dropping 2 or 3 books every step she took. The girl was wearing a pair of incredibly tight jeans and a tube top. She bent over each time to pick up the books! (She didn't merely stoop down to get them!) Two guys saw her and literally ran across the street to help her with the books. Because they were in such a hurry to help the poor, pitiful girl, they almost got hit by an SUV! She stared at them in disbelief.

4. Choose a *familiar quotation* from an essay, book, story, or song that is appropriate to the topic to get your reader's attention: "Hey Shawty, can I have your digits?"

Part B = Thesis

Now that you have your hook, you are ready to tackle Part B, the thesis. We will give an example of how to develop a thesis statement. We will use as a model the #3 Hook above, an anecdote. Considering that the thesis statement is the overriding construct of the essay, we need to choose a statement that will illuminate the issue of women attracting unwanted attention from men. Because the thesis is similar to a contract you make with the reader (that is, you are telling the reader what you will be writing about and are promising to write only about that), the reader will expect you not to renege (go back on) on the agreement.

If we choose as a thesis statement, "I will discuss ways women attract unwanted attention from men in the following paragraphs," this would be a weak, bland, empty thesis statement. Even if it is correct information, we could not develop this statement into a workable, interesting essay. What would be a stronger thesis in regard to our topic, then? To create a solid thesis statement, we need to include not only the topic of women attracting attention from men, but also our own position about attitudes toward unwanted attention. Once we have hooked the readers, we need to ensure that they continue reading; therefore, we must develop a forceful thesis statement such as the following:

ALTHOUGH WOMEN MAY NOT BE AWARE OF IT, THERE ARE WAYS IN WHICH THEY ATTRACT UNWANTED ATTENTION FROM MEN.

SAMPLE INTRODUCTION

On my way to class, I saw a girl get out of her car. She was trying to stack six or eight books and notebooks in her arms, and she kept dropping 2or 3 books every step she took. The girl was wearing a pair of incredibly tight jeans and a tube top. She bent over each time to pick up the books! (She didn't merely stoop down to get them!) Two guys saw her and literally ran across the street to help her with the books. Because they were in such a hurry to help the poor, pitiful girl, they almost got hit by an SUV! She stared at them in disbelief. Like her, most young women aren't aware of why they attract unwanted attention from men.

WRITING THE BODY PARAGRAPH

The next step in the process of building the essay is writing fully-developed body paragraphs that support your thesis. To write a coherent essay, the paragraphs that make up the body of the paper must relate to the thesis. A natural, logical development comes about because you stay true to the same topic while you write more and more detail.

One way to fully develop the topic is to visualize the ideas you have about the topic. Perhaps you can visualize your friend flirting at a fraternity party or visualize men on a street corner whistling at a girl in a short skirt. After you have the image in your head, you transfer it to words on the paper. Then, when others read your words, they will be able to create in their heads the identical picture you had in your head. In order to produce a word-picture, you need to be aware of the features of "full development" and that these features should emerge simultaneously while you are writing a body paragraph. These features are included in the formula below:

BODY PARAGRAPH = TOPIC SENTENCE + SUPPORT SENTENCES

A. *Topic Sentence*. A topic sentence states the central point of a paragraph, in the case of an essay, a body paragraph. It must introduce what you are going to discuss in that body paragraph. A topic sentence is related to the thesis. Look back at Step IV. We listed the three concepts (evidence) that supported the topic. Because they are related to the thesis, they can be turned into topic sentences for our body paragraphs.

Here is our sample Thesis:

Although women may not be aware of it, there are ways in which they attract unwanted attention from men.

Here are our three Concepts related to the Thesis.

    I. Ways Women Dress

    II. Ways Women Behave

    III. Ways Men Respond to Signals from Women

Let's write a Topic Sentence for Concept I, Ways Women Dress.

    Topic Sentence I: *Young women do wear short and revealing clothes.*

Now, you write the Topic Sentences for Concepts II and III.

Topic Sentence II for second concept, Ways Women Behave:

_____

_____

Topic Sentence III for third concept, Ways Men Respond to Signals:

_____

_____

    Two other points to remember about the topic sentence is that a *topic sentence* is usually the first sentence in the paragraph, and 2) it is usually the most broadly stated sentence in the paragraph.

Remember: the topic sentence can appear at the beginning, middle, or end of the body paragraph.

B. Support Sentences. Support sentences directly connect to the topic sentence. Remember that your overall task is to transfer an accurate image from your mind to the printed page. In other words, you must describe graphically, *not tell,* to create a picture of the topic sentence. Therefore, after you have written the topic sentence, the remainder of the body paragraph is several sentences of graphic detail and examples (i.e., your anecdotes) that support the topic sentence. In other words, the remaining sentences will contain a list of specific and similar information related to the topic sentence. Here is a detail sentence relating to Topic Sentence I.

They wear short shorts, tight jeans, cropped tops, and form-fitting dresses.

Now, you write a detail sentence for the topic sentence you wrote for Ways Women Behave.

_____

_____

Last, write a detail sentence for the topic sentence you wrote for Ways Men Respond to Signals.

_____

_____

To flesh out your body paragraph even more, you now add your anecdotes (just refer back to your outline for your "stories"). Here are the example sentences (anecdotes) relating to Topic Sentence I taken from our outline.

For example, in high school during my senior year, a group of popular girls used to wear the tightest clothes, especially sweaters.

On my way to class, I saw a girl get out of her car. She was trying to stack six or eight books and notebooks in her arms. The girl was wearing some incredibly tight jeans and a tube top.

Now, take a look at what we have written for Body Paragraph I so far.

Young women do wear short and revealing clothes. They wear short shorts, cropped tops, tight jeans, and form-fitting dresses. For example, in high school during my senior year, a group of popular girls used to wear the tightest clothes (especially sweaters). On my way to class one chilly morning, I saw a girl get out of her car. She was trying to stack six or eight books and notebooks in her arms. The girl was wearing some incredibly tight jeans and a tube top!

After reading our first body paragraph above, you see that it includes all of the steps in the outline. However, the paragraph is quite bland, not very engaging–really boring. Remember, keeping the reader's attention is a major objective. So, we need to make the essay more interesting by adding a few more sentences. Read the paragraph below. Is it more appealing for the reader? (The new sentences are italicized for your convenience.)

Young women today wear short and revealing clothes. *The retail store racks are filled with clothes that are form-fitting, cropped, or mini-length. Young women from about eighteen to twenty-four buy everything off these racks as soon as the stock arrives. Back in high school Mom, or Dad for that matter, made comments like "Where are you going in that short skirt?" "You don't think I'm buying that tight skirt, do you?" These same girls (now young women) can explore fashions with a freedom they may not have enjoyed before, and they may not consider the way they dress to be provocative. Men, on the other hand, believe that by dressing the way they do, young women call attention to themselves.* For example, in high school during my senior year, a group of popular girls used to wear the tightest clothes, especially sweaters, *and all the guys used to stare at them when they walked by. The boys would hoot and whistle, and beg for dates or phone numbers.*

It's your turn. You write example sentences (anecdotes) for Topic Sentence II, for Ways Women Behave.
_____
_____
_____
_____
_____

You write a body paragraph beginning with your Topic Sentence II.
_____
_____
_____
_____
_____
_____
_____
_____

Write example sentences (anecdotes) for Topic Sentence III, for Ways Men Respond to Signals.
_____
_____
_____
_____
_____

You write a body paragraph beginning with your Topic Sentence III.

WRITING THE CONCLUSION

Once you have completed the body paragraphs, the last step is to bring the essay to a close. The conclusion is the last paragraph of the essay where you give your final opinions about the original topic. You see, in your body paragraphs you investigated several instances or explanations that showed your original opinion, your thesis, to be valid. At the end, you bring the reader full circle, drawing the reader back by revisiting the thesis.

Topic: *Ways Women Attract Unwanted Attention from Men*

Thesis: *Although women may not be aware of it, there are ways they attract unwanted attention from men.*

Body 1: *Ways Women Dress*
Body 2: *Ways Women Behave*

POSSIBLE CONCLUSION: *Men misinterpret women's dress or behavior.*

TO BUILD YOUR CONCLUSION:

1) Write a comment that will stay with the reader;
2) Write a final supporting detail or example; or
3) Write a final forceful but brief argument

---

1) Write a comment that will stay with the reader.

Some women are slaves to present-day fashion and wear form-fitting dresses. Some use female charms and flirt outrageously. Still others may not conduct themselves modestly at parties. However, in each case, men misinterpret women's dress or behavior and approach them with unwanted attention.

2) Write a final supporting detail or example.

Because young women are wearing short shorts and baby tees (cropped tee shirts), men turn towards them whistling and shouting obnoxious comments like, "Hey baby, come to papa!" "Hot stuff! Can I have your number?" This is not an uncommon occurrence. If young women do not want to attract this kind of attention, then perhaps they need to rethink what they wear.

3) Write a final forceful, but brief, argument

So, even though some women may wear everything from hip jeans to a shirt that has a single button at the navel, most women do not want to draw that kind of attention.

Because readers generally spend less than three minutes reading an essay, it is not necessary to repeat the introduction verbatim in the conclusion. However, you may want to restate the thesis. In this instance, use synonyms to retain the same ideas.

Name_____Date_____Score_____

PRACTICE EXIT EXAM: OUTLINE AND ESSAY

Here is your assigned topic: *SCHOOL SHOOTINGS: THE NEW REALITY*

You will want to get on the Internet and find articles related to this topic. Print them out so that you can work from them. Be sure to create a Reference List of your sources.

Step 1: Ask initial questions.

Write your questions on the lines provided.

1._____

2._____

3._____

4._____

5._____

Step 2: Organize the evidence and information by jotting down notes.

HINT: Your outline will depend on the questions you came up with in *Step I.*

Inductive: List ideas you want to write about and examples from what you brainstormed in Step I and what you found on the Internet.

_____

_____

_____

_____

Step 3: Link present information with prior knowledge.
Write anecdotes about a situation that happened to you or something you observed. Recall incidents from public/private school years, present campus life, television reports, etc.

External experience

_____

_____

_____

Previous Personal Experience

_____

_____

_____

Present Personal Experience

_____

_____

_____

Step 4: *Now, review your steps* to see how well the pieces fit into an outline. Sketch out a brief outline below in the spaces provided. Follow these steps: 1) Begin with the two general topics that relate to school shootings. Write them under I and II; 2) Then add the examples developed in Step II that narrowed the topic somewhat. Write them next to (A, B.); 3) Finally, write the specific anecdotes you wrote in Step III (1.,2.).

I.

    A.

        1.

        2.

        3.

II.

    B.

        1.

        2.

        3.

You have successfully planned out your essay and you are ready to begin building the essay. This pre-writing strategy solves several anxieties (worries). First, this outline gives you the whole frame to develop your essay. You will avoid writer's block (you know where you are going and which direction you are going). Second, you already have separate points for each body paragraph. You will avoid writing repetition. Third, you already have supporting examples that are clear and complete. Now, you can move on to Step 5, and write the essay.

Write the Essay: *SCHOOL SHOOTINGS: THE NEW REALITY*

Write the Introduction (Introduction= Hook + Thesis)

_____

_____

_____

_____

_____

Write Body Paragraph 1 (Body Paragraph=topic sentence+support sentences)

*Topic sentence*_____

_____

_____

Support sentences (specific details and examples)_____

_____

_____

_____

_____

_____

_____

_____

_____

Write Body Paragraph 2 (Body Paragraph=topic sentence+support sentences)

Topic Sentence _____

_____

_____

Support Sentences(specific details and examples) _____

_____

_____

_____

_____

_____

_____

_____

If you have a Body Paragraph 3, write it here.

_____

_____

_____

_____

_____

_____

Write the Conclusion (Conclusion=restatement, final anecdote, or final argument)

_____

_____

_____

_____

_____

_____

_____

CHAPTER SEVEN: TYPES OF ESSAYS

At the beginning of the chapter on "Writing the Exit Essay," it was established that you can draw on your prior knowledge to write: you already have a great amount of experience about how to use language–speaking, reading, and writing. So for this chapter on "Writing Types of Essays," you will be able to draw from your reading comprehension experience. You probably have the ability to recognize patterns of organization (i.e., the relationships between ideas that the author uses to organize the writing). Through reading passages and textbook chapters (and looking for key words and phrases in paragraphs), you can identify which pattern the writer uses to develop his/her ideas.

Let's analyze this brief passage to determine the pattern of organization. Choose from Description, Example, Contrast, and Persuasion.

> Television is often a focal point of parental concern. Parents may feel guilty, thinking that their child spends too much time watching television. *On the other hand*, parents often encourage their children to watch educational TV programs such as "Sesame Street." *However* researchers also point out that if any benefits are to be accrued from watching television, the child must watch television with a parent or another caregiver.
>
> –Zigler, p. 347

The italicized words show there is a difference between the three ideas. That is, *On the other hand* lets us know that parents' feelings differ depending on the TV shows their children watch. The contrast word, *However*, tells us that educational programs only benefit the child if the parent also watches. Thus the pattern of organization is contrast.

Exercise 1. Do you know other words that show difference or contrast? Write as many as you can.

_____

_____

Exercise 2. Analyze the following passages. Underline the words or phrases that specify the patterns of organization. Then write them on the line provided. Also note what the pattern is.

A. Encouraging people to diet, to count calories, and to eat healthily by selling "the one plan that works," has been around for a long, long time. For instance, William Gladstone believed people should use a lot of energy to chew all their food, even liquids like soup and milk. He recommended "2 chews per morsel, one for each tooth in a normal mouth." Another example is Horace Fletcher, who faithfully practiced Gladstone's advice by noisily chewing one meal a day. A more recognizable illustration is Dr. Lulu Peters who introduced "calories" to dieters, especially women. She prescribed "self-denial" and "self discipline" *forever.* Finally, William Hay and Gaylord Hauser come on the scene solely to make money. Hay operated a special weight loss resort and Gaylord produced special foods. These nutritionists demonstrated the "semi-scientific hustle"

—Jackson, p. 331-33

B. Even during his boyhood, Granville T. Woods valued the opinions of those genuinely concerned about him. However, he felt he could achieve his goals by himself. He was very sure of what he wanted his future career to be and willing to work hard to achieve it. Yet the trouble was that no one believed in him. Everyone thought that if he left school to find apprentice work, his education would end. Granville had to prove it the hard way. Contrary to their doubts, in 1887, Woods became famous by inventing the induction telegraph system, which eliminated train collisions.

—Shepard, p. 35-40

C. Cigarette smoking kills 307,000 people in the United States each year. Lung cancer and emphysema (chronic lung disease) are the best known and among the most miserable outcomes. Smoking atherosclerosis develops faster, and affects smokers even worse than the other diseases mentioned. Atherosclerosis results in heart attacks and strokes, heart pains, leg pains, and many other problems. Pipe and cigar smoking don't have the pulmonary (lung) consequences that cigarette smoking does, but can lead to cancer of the lips, tongue, and esophagus. Nicotine in any form has bad effects on the small blood vessels and thus increases your chance of heart attacks.

—Vickery, p.13

D. Self confidence in that way he did not lack. He had fine black hair over very blue eyes and a fresh complexion. He was slim, very slightly built; and all his movements were neat and trim, though with a tendency to a certain grandiose exaggeration of one or two of Charles' physical mannerisms that he thought particularly gentlemanly. Women's eyes seldom left him at the first glance, but from closer acquaintance with London girls he had never got much beyond a reflection of his own cynicism.

—Fowles, p. 141

> Key words help you determine whether the writer is contrasting, describing, persuading, or illustrating when you read a passage. You can apply this same understanding when you write your essay. Just like you unraveled the intent or purpose in the reading passages by determining what type of passages they were, you can now use key words and patterns to put together your ideas to write an excellent essay.

When you are given a writing assignment, sometimes the topic is stated in such a way that a hint or clue is given. This clue gives you a pattern of organization to respond to. For instance, your instructor may ask you "to describe the most desolate or dreary place you've ever visited." The word "describe" is the clue that shapes your essay. You are aware that you must use the descriptive pattern of organization.

Exercise 3. Read these topics below and in the space provided write the pattern of organization each topic suggests.

1. What is one difference between traditional shopping and shopping on-line?

2. Discuss some of the worst things that people do to one another.

3. "Americans are too dependent on the automobile." Attack or defend.

4. Write about the characteristics of an honorable person.

5. "High schools put too much emphasis on athletics." Attack or defend.

6. Write about a popular horror film that you enjoyed watching.

7. "Evil, like good, has its own heroes." Who are some characters from movies you consider to be "evil heroes?"

8. What is different about going to the theater and staying at home to watch a movie?

In writing, the term used for patterns of organization is "rhetorical modes." "Rhetorical modes" means the style or method the writer uses to shape ideas, like the writers did in the passages above. Traditionally there are ten modes, types, or ways to write, but for our purposes, we will concentrate only on four.

Description is a strategy that creates a concrete image or detailed picture of a person, place, object, thing, or idea. To help you gather a set of details, use the sensory technique by describing the sound, taste, texture, color, or aroma. Also use adjectives and adverbs because they describe nouns and verbs. Through your writing, try to help the reader visualize what you are writing about.

Example is a strategy that uses different instances that fit a general idea or incident. For example, you can write a set of specifics: people, places, dates, statistics, actions, and so on to represent (explain) the thesis. Examples you use in a body paragraph should support the thesis as well as your topic sentence. Use key words and phrases like *for example, for instance, such as, like, as, to illustrate, etc.*

Contrast is a strategy that shows how two or more (but usually two) subjects are different. Point out how each subject is unlike the other by using key words and phrases like *yet, but, opposite, on the contrary, whereas, on the other hand, though, although, by contrast, however, differ, different, etc.*

Persuasion is a strategy that offers an opinion about an issue--explanations supported by facts. In order to get your point across, use strong language that stacks evidence on one side.

Exercise 4. Read the essay topics below. Select an appropriate rhetorical mode from the list above, and write your choice in the space provided.

1. What problems develop when people change to eating fast food?

2. What are the qualities of good music?

3. What frightened you as a child that you find amusing now?

4. What is the most frustrating day you have had recently?

5. Movie ratings are useful and accurate.

6. What are the best ways to deal with telephone solicitors?

7. Discuss, respectively, the merits of toddlers going to daycare or staying at home.

8. Write about your impressions of a place you visited as a child and returned to visit as an adult.

9. Children need to believe in Santa Claus.

10. Choose three movie stars who serve as role models for our youth.

> Now you can see that reading for patterns of organization is similar to using rhetorical modes when writing.

WRITING DESCRIPTIVE ESSAYS

Writing an essay that uses description as the rhetorical mode means that you will bring to life a person, place, thing, idea, object, or action through a word-picture. Therefore, you should choose words that project a concrete (actual, touchable) image of the picture for your reader. To create this specific image, you can draw upon your five senses: touch, smell, sight, hearing, and taste. If you were describing the worst meal you ever ate, you would use taste, smell (aroma), and sight (color). You might use sound (crunchy) or touch/texture (gritty on the tongue). Also, enhancing your essay by sprinkling a good number of vivid adjectives and adverbs throughout will liven up nouns and active verbs.

For descriptive essays, don't forget to use the following:

DESCRIPTIVE ESSAY	=	A. lots of adjectives and adverbs
		B. uses the five senses

Let's create an introduction and develop a descriptive body paragraph to demonstrate. The topic is THE WORST MEAL I EVER ATE.

Introduction

I have eaten many meals that were neither wholesome nor complete. Often I have made a meal simply from a mayonnaise sandwich, or just a handful of candy-coated peanuts and a soft drink. A few times my entire meal consisted of chocolate cookies and red punch. (*Thesis*) Even though there wasn't much nutritional value in those meals, I would rather have those than what an ex-roommate in college cooked for me a week ago. That was the worst meal I have ever eaten.

Exercise 1. What do you think the "hook" is for this introduction?

Body Paragraph

Because this ex-roommate ate many dinners I prepared for her at my house, I was quite happy when she finally invited me to eat a meal at her apartment. When I walked in the door, I was immediately overwhelmed by an aroma that smelled like the home-cooked meals my mother served. As I anxiously waited to eat, I dreamed up all kinds of delicious foods that might soon be forthcoming: mounds of fluffy mashed potatoes dented with pools of smooth, seasoned gravy, golden fried pork chops, creamy macaroni, crisp green beans, buttery corn-on-the-cob, tiny lima beans, and on and on. Finally, I was escorted to my seat at the table. My friend had laid out her best china, crystal, and silver. I was allowed to fill my plate first with fried chicken, rice and gravy, green beans, corn-on-the-cob and, you guessed it, creamy macaroni! I dug in and scooped up a fork full of macaroni and shoved that in my mouth; then, I bit into the crunchy fried chicken. Then I got the shock of my life. My face became flushed; I grabbed my glass and gulped down the tea. I had never, ever, eaten food that tasted like an entire box of salt had been dumped onto every morsel. The inside of my mouth, tongue, and throat burned and felt raw. I was light-headed and just knew I was having an attack. I began to cough hysterically and didn't stop for a full three minutes. I begged off and got out of there as fast as I could.

STOP! Please remember that for the exit essay you will need to write *at least two body paragraphs*. The body paragraph above was created to give you an idea of how to write one well-developed body paragraph. ALSO REMEMBER THAT YOU WILL BE REQUIRED TO WRITE A CONCLUSION FOR THE EXIT ESSAY.

Exercise 2a. Underline the adjectives that make the description of the meal so vivid. Write them here.

_____

_____

_____

Exercise 2b. Name the senses that are evident throughout the body paragraph, and then give examples of the words/phrases used to illustrate them.

_____

_____

_____

_____

Exercise 3. Now, you try. Your topic is "The Worst Date I Ever Had." Depending upon the format you choose for the introduction, write the thesis statement either at the beginning or at the end of your paragraph.

Introduction
(*Thesis*) _____

_____

_____

 Or (*Thesis*) _____

Body Paragraph
A. Before you begin to write your body paragraph, write a list of adjectives you want to use to describe your date (the person), the place you went, and what happened there.

_____ _____ _____ _____

B. Now, begin your paragraph.

Exercise 4.

Here is a second topic for practice: "Describe Your Ideas of Feminine or Masculine Beauty." Depending upon the format you choose for the introduction, write the thesis statement either at the beginning or at the end of your paragraph.

Introduction
(*Thesis*)

Or (*Thesis*) _____

Body Paragraph
A. Before you begin to write your body paragraph, write a list of adjectives you want to use to describe your ideas about feminine or masculine beauty.

_____   _____   _____

_____   _____   _____

_____   _____   _____

_____

B. Now, begin your paragraph.

_____

_____

_____

_____

_____

_____

_____

_____

_____

_____

_____

_____

WRITING AN EXAMPLE ESSAY

Writing an essay that uses examples as the rhetorical mode involves a three-step process.

Step 1. The first step is to determine the idea you want to get across.

Step 2. Next, within the introduction, write a thesis that focuses on your idea.

Step 3. The third step is to develop each body paragraph using specific examples of your idea: names, places, dates, facts, and so on. If you prefer, you can write a strong example that is a brief anecdote/narrative, which tells who, what, when, where, and why or how. Be sure you use accurate nouns and varied action verbs. Finally, always make sure that your examples are credible and relevant to the thesis.

When you write an example essay, be sure to include some of these words and phrases:

| for example | for instance | such as | to illustrate |
| to demonstrate | specifically | like | portrayal |

Let's write an introduction and body paragraph to demonstrate the use of example. The topic is "Give Examples of How to Get Out of a Speeding Ticket."

Introduction
   Speeding fines are quite expensive. No one likes being charged fifty dollars or three hundred dollars for one driving violation. It seems amazing that you could possibly be charged $150 for going ten miles over the posted speed limit. So, some people will try any trick or give any excuse to avoid getting the citation. THESIS: From saying that they are in crisis to saying they are on their way to church services, people seem to think they have the "perfect excuse" for speeding.

Body Paragraph
   I have heard plenty of stories about people getting away with speeding. When it comes to avoiding a speeding ticket, they use anything and anyone: medical excuses, children, and the elderly. For example, being sick usually generates sympathy from even the sternest police officer. Consider this scenario: the officer pulls over a car. The dad tells his child to bend over, grab her stomach, and cry. When the officer approaches the driver, the dad pleads that they are on their way to the emergency room because "his little princess" has stomach pains. To illustrate further, there's the guy who hasn't paid his last ticket, so he may say his wife/girlfriend is pregnant and suffering a miscarriage. Another good instance is the nervous mom who says she has to rush to the pharmacy because her child (or grandmother) "needs the medication immediately!" An example of a college student's excuse may be just as convincing. The guy declares his roommate is deathly ill, and he is even skipping class to get medicine until his buddy's parent gets there. If none of these "good reasons" comes to mind, then the driver can

always use this lame excuse, "I just started to feel bad and I wanted to get home while I could still drive myself. I have no one else to help me."

Exercise 1a.
Underline the actual examples used in the paragraph above. Write them here.
_____
_____
_____
_____

Exercise 1b.
Write the key words that indicate example.
_____
_____

Exercise 1c.
Write the specific nouns/action verbs/ adjectives that are in at least two of the examples above.
_____
_____
_____

Another Example Essay (same topic using one anecdote)

Introduction
     Probably only a few lucky people have gotten out of a speeding ticket despite the number of years they have driven, the many states they have driven in, and the speed they have driven. However, I have never been that lucky and have paid several fines over the years.
THESIS: Still, I have always wondered if there is such a thing as "the perfect excuse" for getting out of a speeding ticket.

Arthur and Pate — Page 248

Body Paragraph

Speeding most often occurs when driving long distances on interstate highways or rushing to an appointment across town. When the state patrol officer pulls up behind the driver, blue lights flashing and sirens screaming loudly, rarely do drivers calmly pull over and accept the citation gracefully. Most of the time, drivers desperately try to think of that one perfect excuse because they just don't want to pay the fine. An example of this was the time my sister and I were driving through Mississippi on the way back to Georgia. It was her turn to drive for three hours, and she was going about 80 mph when we saw the patrol car. Because the patrol officer turned around in the grassy median, we panicked and just knew that the fine was going to be more than we could afford. Well, she was very nervous as she pulled over on the shoulder because the car had Georgia plates, and she had a Massachusetts' driver's license. We had always heard that if a driver had out-of-state plates or license that the fine would be higher. Since we were in a no-win situation on both counts, we knew we were in big trouble. The officer wanted to know where we were going in such a hurry. She said we had to get back to Georgia because we received word that our mother was ill. She had just taken our sister and two little children back to Louisiana because our sister had no car. And when we dropped her off, we received an emergency call and were trying to get back as soon as we could. Well, that did no good; she still got a ticket. However, she pled her case in traffic court in Massachusetts and didn't have to pay the fine. I guess my sister had the perfect excuse after all.

STOP! Please remember that for the exit essay you will need to write AT LEAST TWO body paragraphs. The body paragraph above was created to give you an idea of how to write one well-developed body paragraph. ALSO REMEMBER THAT YOU WILL BE REQUIRED TO WRITE A CONCLUSION FOR THE EXIT ESSAY.

Exercise 2a.
How is this essay different from the first?

_____

_____

_____

Exercise 2b.
Write the specific nouns/action verbs/ adjectives that make the anecdote lively.

_____

_____

Exercise 2c.
Write a summary of an anecdote about getting out of a speeding ticket.
_____

_____

_____

Exercise 3.
Now you try an example essay on your own. Your topic is "The Excuses People Give for Skipping Class." Before you begin, list the examples you will use here.

_____   _____

_____   _____

If you are going to use one anecdote as your example, write it here.

_____

_____

_____

Depending upon the format you choose for the introduction, write the thesis statement either at the beginning or at the end of your paragraph.

Introduction
(*Thesis*) _____

_____

_____

or (*Thesis*) _____

Body Paragraph (your choice)
_____

_____

Body Paragraph, continued

_____
_____
_____
_____
_____
_____

Exercise 4.
Here is another practice exercise. Your topic is "Instances When Telling a Lie Is the Best Thing." Before you begin, list the examples you will use here.

_____   _____

_____   _____

If you are going to use one anecdote as your example, write it here.
_____
_____
_____

Depending upon the format you choose for the introduction, write the thesis statement either at the beginning or at the end of your paragraph.

Introduction
(*Thesis*) _____
_____
_____

or (*Thesis*) _____

Body Paragraph (your choice)

_____

_____

_____

_____

_____

_____

_____

_____

WRITING PERSUASIVE ESSAYS

Using persuasion as the rhetorical mode involves convincing your reader that your opinion concerning a particular issue is solid. Since your opinion is just your view or belief, you must present facts to back up your opinion. This means you provide statistics, definitions, specific cases (names, dates, places), quotes from experts, and so forth. Clearly, any information that would support the opposite side would not be helpful to your case; therefore, for a persuasive essay you intentionally omit information that argues against you; in other words, stack the deck on one side – your side.

For the persuasive essay, be sure to

PERSUASIVE ESSAYS	=	A. STACK SUPPORT ON YOUR SIDE B. USE STRONG WORDS AND PHRASES

The paragraphs below are an introduction and a body paragraph which were created to illustrate how to write a persuasive essay. The topic is *COLLEGE ATHLETES SHOULD STAY IN SCHOOL*.

| Arthur and Pate | Page 252 |

Introduction

A few years ago, just about every young boy interested in basketball wanted to grow up to be Michael Jordan. Today, players enjoying such celebrity are Alonzo Mourning, Kobe Bryant, Grant Williams, and Jason Garnett. All of these famous athletes stayed in college and graduated before joining professional teams. *THESIS:* Although many college athletes are just as talented and could easily drop out of school, I strongly believe they should finish their degree and receive their diploma before joining a professional team.

Exercise 1. What do you believe to be the "hook" for this introduction? Write it here.

___

Body Paragraph

All sports have an inherent drawback; the players are subject to injury. They sprain or break every part of the body: knee, foot, hand, wrist, ankle, shoulder, neck, hip, and back. Just listen to the sports reports. "A sprained right ankle landed reserve Cedric Henderson on the injured list February 15th and will keep him out indefinitely. SF Rice has not played since December 6th because of a partially torn tendon. A recent MRI on the injury showed no improvement, so Rice had surgery to correct the problem on January 7th, and is likely done for the year. Starzz guard and former UConn standout Shea Ralph underwent successful knee surgery for the fifth time." From football to hockey to women's basketball, professional players suffer serious injuries that disable them time and time again. Pretty soon "out for the season" becomes "out of a sports career." What if the injury occurred during the first year of being signed? Then where is the huge salary, where are the endorsements, and where is the fame? When a player is out of the lime light, he or she is out of the news, out of fans' minds, and out of luck. Without another career that the forgotten athletes prepared for in college, what do they have to fall back on?

> **STOP!** Please remember that for the exit essay you will need to write *at least two* body paragraphs. The body paragraph above was created to give you an idea of how to write one well-developed body paragraph. ALSO REMEMBER THAT YOU WILL BE REQUIRED TO WRITE A CONCLUSION FOR THE EXIT ESSAY.

Exercise 2a. Take a look at the introduction. Write is the writer's opinion? Write the rationale used to persuade the reader of the opinion found in the introduction.

Exercise 2b. Take a look at the body paragraph and determine how the "deck is stacked." Write the evidence here.

Exercise 2c. Find the facts, examples, or quotes that support the writer's opinion. Write them here.

_____

_____

_____

_____

Exercise 3

Now, try this topic: "College Students Should Marry after Graduating." Depending upon the format you choose for the introduction, write the thesis statement either at the beginning or at the end of your paragraph.

Introduction

(*Thesis*) _____

_____

_____

or (*Thesis*) _____

Body Paragraph (Include rationale as well as support)

_____

_____

Exercise 4.

Write another practice introduction and body paragraph for this topic: "Is Ecstasy Harmful? Why or Why Not?" Choose one side. Depending upon the format you choose for the introduction, write the thesis statement at the beginning or at the end of your paragraph.

Introduction

(*Thesis*) _____

_____

or (*Thesis*) _____

Body Paragraph (Include rationale and support)

_____
_____
_____
_____
_____
_____
_____

WRITING CONTRAST ESSAYS

Contrast is a rhetorical mode that explains the difference between two (or more) subjects. However, the two subjects being discussed need to belong to the same topic. For example, *Halloween* and *Child's Play* belong to the same topic–horror movies. And *rap* and *hard rock* belong to the same topic, music.

Step 1. Brainstorm

The first step in a contrast essay is to look at items, persons, or ideas within your thesis and choose two subjects that belong to it. Let's work with this topic: *THE DIFFERENCES BETWEEN AMUSEMENT PARKS*. Since "amusement parks" is the topic, let's choose two popular parks: Disney World and Six Flags Over Georgia.

Step 2. Write the introduction

Next, you will write the introduction. Most contrast essays have similar introductions in that they merely state what the writer will be contrasting. An example for the thesis for our topic is "Yet, each amusement park is unique and different." Keep in mind that you want to use a "hook" to captivate your reader.

Step 3. Write a body paragraph

The third step then is to select points or characteristics that both amusement parks have. For instance, each park has [1] location, [2] size, [3] rides, and so on.

Exercise 1a.

Can you think of any more points or features about amusement parks? Write them here.

_____

_____

Step 4. Choose a plan of organization

Last, within the body paragraph, you need to explain points or characteristics about each subject, Disney World and Six Flags. The explanation (or description) must pinpoint the differences only. You do *not*, in a contrast essay, talk about how the subjects are the same. For example, one characteristic about both parks is "location." Even though each park has a "location" characteristic, the description of each location will show a difference, a contrast: Disney World is located in central Florida, and Six Flags Over Georgia is located in northern Georgia.

> NOTE: If both parks were located in Atlanta, you would not choose to talk about location. You would have to choose something else to discuss in your body paragraph.

Exercise 1b. Explain the next characteristic, "size", for each park and pinpoint the difference.

_____

_____

Step 5. Finally, decide on the format of your body paragraphs that will best show the differences between the two subjects. The two usual patterns are (A) *block* and (B) *alternate*. *Block* organization means to develop the first subject characteristics in its entirety. Then, you will move to the second topic and develop it and all its characteristics.

BLOCK: (x= Disney World, y= Six Flags)

    Introduction

        A. Body Paragraph on x

            1. **Location:** Disney World is located in Orlando, Florida.

            2. **Size:** This huge complex consists of five separate theme parks that attract thousands a day.

            3. **Rides:** Each theme park has several rides specifically designed for its theme, from the Magic Carpet of Aladdin at Magic Kingdom to Twilight Zone Tower of Terror at MGM Studios to Kilimanjaro Safaris at Animal Kingdom.

(transition words between Paragraph A and Paragraph B) *On the other hand,*

        B. Body Paragraph on Y

            1. **Location:** Six Flags is located in north Georgia, specifically, Atlanta, Georgia.

            2. **Size:** This popular amusement park is smaller, as it is only one park.

            3. **Rides:** Hundreds of guests attend to ride on the main attractions: roller coasters like Georgia Scorcher and the recent Superman-Ultimate Flight and kiddie rides like Little Aviator.

The introduction and body paragraph below illustrate how the BLOCK outline is utilized to write a contrast essay:

Introduction

     Amusement parks are very popular sources of recreation for the whole family. This is one of the main reasons you see huge crowds of parents, grandparents, teens, children, and infants swarm to these places like "white on rice." Disney World and Six Flags Over Georgia are two highly frequented parks, and many people have been to both.
THESIS: Yet each amusement park is unique and different.

Body Paragraph

     The first difference is that Disney World is located in sunny Orlando, Florida and draws in thousands of people a day. Most people think of the Magic Kingdom as comprising Disney World in its entirety. In reality, the complex has several enormous, individual theme parks that cover quite a few miles. The Disney complex also includes Epcot, MGM Studios, Animal Kingdom, and Pleasure Island which have several rides that fit its own special theme. Epcot, with futuristic experiences as its theme, features Body Wars and Test Track. Magic Kingdom is the ultimate fairy tale come-to-life: Aladdin's Magic Carpet and Buzz Lightyear Space Ranger Spin. On the other hand, Six Flags Over Georgia, located in cooler northern Georgia, is a single park that covers several acres, not miles. When contrasted to Disney World, this park has only one theme. The attractions are the popular roller-coaster rides: Batman, Scorcher, Cyclone, Mind Bender, and Ninja.

Exercise 2a. Underline the key words that show contrast. Write them here.

_____

_____

Exercise 2b. List points/characteristics being contrasted. Write them here.

Disney World	Six Flags Over Georgia
_____	_____
_____	_____
_____	_____

     The second format, *alternate* organization, involves developing the first point or characteristic by discussing the explanation (or description) of both subjects in the same paragraph and then moving on to develop the second point or characteristic, and so on.

If you choose to write in the Alternating format, your outline will look like this:

ALTERNATING: (X= Disney World, Y= Six Flags)

    Introduction

        A. Body Paragraph on location and size

            1. X= Disney World   (transition words within paragraph)

            2. Y= Six Flags   (transition words within paragraph)

Disney World is further south in Florida, *whereas* Six Flags is north of it in Georgia. Disney World has five separate theme parks that make up a huge complex; *by contrast*, Six Flags is smaller, a single theme park.

        B. Body Paragraph on rides

            1. x= Disney World   (transition words within paragraph)

            2. y= Six Flags   (transition words within paragraph)

Disney World has several theme-specific rides at each of the four parks. For example, Animal Kingdom capitalizes on its theme with rides featuring the prehistoric dinosaur and Kilimanjaro Safaris. *However*, nearly all of Six Flags' adult rides are roller coasters, featuring two popular characters, Superman and Batman.

When writing a contrast essay, be sure to use the following words/phrases:

Key CONTRAST words:	yet	opposite	whereas	however	on the other hand
	but	though	although	by contrast	on the contrary

> **STOP!** Please remember that for the exit essay you will need to write *at least two* body paragraphs. The body paragraph above was created to give you an idea of how to write one well-developed body paragraph. ALSO REMEMBER THAT YOU WILL BE REQUIRED TO WRITE A CONCLUSION FOR THE EXIT ESSAY.

Exercise 3. Choose whether you will write this essay in BLOCK or ALTERNATING style: *THE DIFFERENCES BETWEEN OLDER AND YOUNGER COLLEGE STUDENTS.* Write an introduction and develop a contrast. Depending upon the format you choose for the introduction, write the thesis statement at the beginning or at the end of your paragraph.

Introduction

(*Thesis*)
_____
_____
_____

or (*Thesis*)
_____

Body Paragraph
_____
_____
_____
_____
_____
_____
_____
_____
_____
_____

Exercise 4. Now, you try this topic: *THE DIFFERENCES BETWEEN MALE AND FEMALE BODY LANGUAGE.* Write an introduction and develop a contrast in your body paragraphs. Depending upon the format you choose for the introduction, write the thesis statement at the beginning or at the end of your paragraph.

Introduction

(*Thesis*)
_____
_____
_____

or (*Thesis*)
_____

Body Paragraph
_____
_____
_____
_____
_____
_____
_____
_____
_____
_____

GENERAL GUIDELINES FOR WRITING EXIT ESSAYS

1. Engage the reader's interest.

2. Make a concentrated effort to stay focused on a central idea.

3. Write a clear thesis statement.

4. Use appropriate diction that illustrates that the student has a good command of everyday language.

5. Be organized when considering the content of what you say; your sentences should be relevant to the assigned topic.

6. Inadequate adequate, specific, and relevant support within body paragraphs.

7. Write a variety of sentence structures.

8. Be free of major errors in grammar, punctuation, structure, and usage.

9. Write an essay of adequate length.

SUGGESTED TOPICS FOR TYPES OF ESSAYS

DESCRIPTIVE

1. Describe yourself in terms of being either a "neat freak" or a "pack rat."
2. Describe a particular event in your life that changed your plans.
3. Describe someone in your life that changed your attitude.
4. Describe some experiences while attending college that you have found frustrating.
5. Describe the qualities you consider desirable in a mate.
6. Describe what it is like being in your position in the family (i.e., oldest, middle, youngest, or only child).

EXAMPLE

1. Are you a superstitious person? Give instances that illustrate your belief system.
2. Write an essay on returning (retro) clothing styles.
3. What are some issues couples should agree on before getting married?
4. Who are some villains you like to keep up with on television?
5. Write an essay which focuses on the characteristics of charismatic leaders. Give specific examples.

PERSUASIVE

1. Are there advantages to living in a blended family? Why or why not?
2. Local drinking establishments encourage excessive drinking among college students. Agree or disagree.
3. Should men and women be encouraged to join the military? Why or why not?
4. Beauty pageants reinforce stereotypes of women. Agree or disagree.
5. Playing competitive team sports is dangerous and should be banned. Agree or disagree.

CONTRAST

1. What are some differences between male and female grooming habits?
2. Write about the differences between dating someone from another culture and dating someone from your own culture.
3. What did you expect from your college years? What are your actual experiences?
4. What kinds of things does your mother do that drives you crazy? Is she very different from your father in that regard? (Or use sibling, aunt, uncles, or grandparent.)
5. Contrast two genres of music today.

ANSWER KEYS FOR CHAPTERS
AND PRACTICE EXIT EXAMS

CHAPTER ONE

Answers will vary.

CHAPTER TWO

Exercise 1a. These are suggested answers only. Answers will vary.

1. Not coming in until very early the next morning, Gary was late to work.
2. Margaret found it hard to stay in school with the cost of tuition steadily increasing.
3. The airplane with a ten-million pound capacity flew like a bird in the air.
4. The students danced and danced for two solid hours.
5. Katie saw Enrique and was scared to death.

Exercise 1b.

6. Although Mr. Urteaga is a fine gentleman and close friend, he is untrustworthy in his relationships with women.
7. Why do heathens clamor and fools rage?
8. Right in the middle of her argument with Liberace, Anita actually fell down and cried.
9. I want to be a football star when I grow up and become a big boy.
10. Suzanna and Fabian are always fighting over who wears the most expensive clothes, especially when they find themselves at the same parties.

Exercise 1c.

11. s
12. s
13. f
14. f
15. f
16. s
17. f
18. s
19. s
20. f

Exercise 2a.

1. semester. Kel
2. Up. I

3. together. They
4. without. Others
5. grandmother. She
6. town. It's
7. qualities. What
8. winding. Other
9. sun. Will
10. Others. I

Exercise 2b.
1. deep; I
2. beautiful; Whites
3. delicious; the
4. journey; I
5. books; put
6. sometimes; I
7. ago; he
8. Jayson; they're
9. man; he
10. tonight; romance

Exercise 2c.

1. cobbler, and her
2. relationship, but after
3. together, but they
4. weary, and I
5. class, so I
6. empty, but we're
7. Eric, but Jedidiah
8. heat, so they
9. register, and the
10. again, for the

Exercise 3a.

1. later. or Later I
2. lake. We
3. semester. Last
4. shake. Others
5. believe. It's
6. rain. I
7. dance. John
8. dating. I
9. summer. They
10. rage. Evil

Mastery Exercise

1. (CS) Fabio and Giovanni played basketball all day long; they went to evening church service at 7:00 p.m. (Or long. They)
2. (CS) Scarlett lied about having a date with Melanie's husband, but the two still remained good friends. (Or husband. The) (Or husband; the)
3. (R-O) I tried to find a convenient place to park at the rave, but he said there was parking available on the back lot only. (Or rave. He) (or rave; he)
4. (CS) Earlier in the day I had wanted to party and dance all night. My boyfriend changed my mind. (Or night; my)
5. (R-O) What can I say? I have no explanation for my behavior. I'm just a fool in love! (Or behavior; I'm)
6. (R-O) It's really interesting the way Ebony and Ivory say they love each other more than life itself. They fight and argue all the time. (or ;)
7. (CS) Let's get together for dinner tomorrow evening. I want to get your opinion on something. (Or evening; I)
8. (R-O) When my great grandfather considered that half hi life was spent in a dark world, he wanted to die. Then, his friends talked him out of taking drastic measures.
9. (CS) Next summer I refuse to work. I will go to far away lands as my friend Linda does each year. (Or work; I)
10. (CS) I wish I could get out of this place; the flourescent lights are making me dizzy. (Or place. The)

Exercise 4a.

1. blowing
2. Fallen
3. chosen
4. hang
5. dove
6. shrunk
7. arose
8. brought
9. frozen
10. thrown

Exercise 4b.

Answers will vary.

Exercise 5a.

1. are
2. is
3. was
4. was
5. were

Exercise 6a.

1. . . . but Mary said Sue like it that way.
2. . . . John looked at Peter and James and placed it on Peter's head. Or
   . . . John looked at Peter and James and placed it on James' head.
3. . . . making the mask look even uglier than before. Or
   . . . making his face look even uglier than before.
4. . . . the trees fell to the ground. Or
   . . . Kimiko and Fabio fell to the ground.
5. . . . that Turenda could do anything she wanted to. Or
   . . . that Annise could do anything she wanted to.

Exercise 6b.

1. hers
2. is
3. he or she; he or she; his or her
4. his or her
5. her; them; he or she
6. his or her
7. his or her
8. her
9. , the train crashed. Or
   , the bus crashed.
10. he or she feels

MASTERY TEST ONE

The following are suggested answers. Responses will vary.

1. The door with the broken lock was stuck.
2. After coming home from a night of wild partying, the boys immediately fell asleep.
3. The historian brought up a big issue regarding world peace.
4. The class was nearly over when the students came without their assignments.
5. If carol and sue have to enroll in the same course again, they will just die.

B.

6. man; he
7. other, but they
8. destroy? Why
9. thing; no
10. tonight; it

C.

11. RO
12. RO
13. OK
14. OK
15. RO

D.

16. chosen
17. is
18. buy
19. fall
20. were

E.

21. ...Billy Bob announced that he wanted Margaret Ann... Or
    ...Sue Ellen to leave the party...
22. Herbert told Chris that Chris... Or
    Herbert did not belong...
23. his or her
24. his or her
25. , it seemed as if the stars... Or
    Ian and paddy would fall to the ground

CHAPTER THREE

Exercise 1a.

1. money, jewelry, book collection,
2. skydiving, bungee jumping, sailing,
3. No change
4. Jolene, Kristin, Lamont, Malek,
5. stamp collection, a set of heirloom china. . .,
6. money, owned more . . ., and gave more to . . .
7. weddings, help older people . . ., laugh at others' . . .,
8. Mother Nature, Mother Teresa,
9. airplane, bus, or
10. friends, neighbors,

Exercise 1b.

1. , **but**
2. , **so**
3. , **or**
4. , **and**
5. , **for**
6. , **but**
7. , **but**
8. , **nor**
9. , **yet**
10. , **or**

Exercise 1c.

1. Really,
2. together, the
3. No,
4. pounds, would
5. Yes,
6. classes, you
7. flag, the
8. Somehow,
9. No,
10. home, Manuel

Exercise 1d.

1. morning, I . . . face, eat breakfast, get dressed, walk . . . ,
2. marriage, they
3. Yes, . . ., but
4. class, yet
5. day, my
6. pants, socks,
7. hammer, nails, screwdriver,
8. house, especially the dog, cat, monkey, and
9. better, I'm
10. university, no

Exercise 2a.

Answers will vary.

Exercise 2b.

1. Yes
2. No   Venezuela; his
3. Yes
4. Yes
5. No   cherries, a
6. No   park, a . . .tea, a . . . serenade,
7. Yes
8. No   exam, but
9. Yes
10. No   no, . . . go; I
11. No   warm, cozy . . . ; . . . cool, refreshing . . . lemonade; . . . favorite, suspenseful, captivating
12. Yes
13. No   crazy; my
14. Yes
15. No   me, I

Exercise 3a.

1. crime: guns
2. quality: intelligence
3. year: Denyce
4. spirit: she
5. items: high
6. Juan: mean
7. store: bread
8. these: pens
9. admire: intelligence
10. life: she is

Exercise 4a.

1. anyone's
2. Eddie's
3. students'
4. novel's
5. women's . . . children's
6. men's . . . women's
7. children's
8. Alyss'
9. leaders'
10. anyone's
11. somebody's
12. theirs
13. friend's . . . neighbors'
14. boys'
15. girl's

Exercise 4b.

1. He's
2. weren't
3. I had . . . I would
4. She is . . . I am
5. he is
6. You're
7. cannot
8. I'm
9. She is . . . he has
10. you are

Exercise 4c.

1. 7's...7's
2. 8's...9's
3. R's
4. 4's...6's
5. *their's*
6. 1960's...1970's   Or 1960s...1970s
7. 1700's   Or 1700s
8. V's...U's
9. Ph.D.'s...MA's
10. I's...*tin's*...*ten's*

Exercise 4d.

1. Tyrone lives a very exciting life in Mayberry, North Carolina.
2. Culture studies reveal that most North Carolinians are much happier people than Midwesterners.
3. Many children don't even care about making A's in school.

MASTERY TEST TWO

1. No   running, looked..., and
2. No   testify, the   Or   optional comma
3. No   well; I   Or   well: I   Or   well. I
4. No   choices, including...following: airplane, car, boat, and
5. No   houses, cars, jewelry, and
6. Yes
7. Yes
8. No   school, Jennifer..."nerds;" Jesse   Or   "nerds." Jesse
9. Yes
10. No   day; tomorrow   Or   day. Tomorrow
11. Yes
12. No   Sure,
13. No   succeed, try
14. No   sex, drugs, and
15. Yes
16. No   met: hell..., donkeys..., and
17. No   drive; we're   Or   drive. We're
18. Yes
19. No   Orlando, Atlanta, Savannah, and
20. No   name; everything   Or   name. Everything

21. No	breakfast, . . . bacon, eggs, ham, cheese, and	
22. No	smart, but	
23. Yes		
24. No	all: looks, talent, fame, fortune, and	
25. No	product, ask . . .; you'll Or product, ask . . . back. You'll	
26. No	relationship: an	
27. Yes	(optional: was; people)	
28. Yes		
29. Yes		
30. No	don't . . . reasons: lack . . . , plenty . . . , and	
31. No	, it Or optional comma	
32. No	dogs, not pigs and goats	
33. No	Italy, and	
34. No	yes, . . .; they Or yes, . . . culprits. They	
35. No	grades, their . . . increase. They . . . , and . . . happy, proud, and	
36. No	she's	
37. No	brain's	
38. No	children's	
29. No	farmers' Or farmer's	
40. Yes		
41. No	money, fame, nor	
42. No	sleep, and	
43. No	music, but	
44. No	luck: . . . job, . . . home, . . . family,	
45. No	horse, get	
46. No	courses, teachers	
47. No	No, . . . ; they Or crime. They	
48. No	him; he Or him. He	
49. Yes		
50. No	year, I	

CHAPTER FOUR

Exercise 1a. These are suggested answers. Responses will vary.

1. Standing on a hill, Miss Martin watched the stars.
2. Not surprisingly, the highway was jammed with traffic during the holidays.
3. I am tired, especially tonight.   Or   I am especially tired tonight.
4. Only time will tell whether Jim and Suellyn will rekindle their friendship.   Or   Time will tell whether Jim and Suellyn will only rekindle their friendship.

| Arthur and Pulley | Page 277 |

5. Just the charge for the drapes and the kitchen appliances is included in the cost.
   Or   The charge for the drapes and the kitchen appliances is included in just the cost.
6. On the average, football coaches earn more money than drama coaches.
7. Marissa refused to marry Maurice after she learned of his obvious affairs.
   Obviously, Marissa refused to marry Maurice after she learned of his affairs.
8. With their eyes tightly closed, David and Roger talked with their dead wives.
9. Generally, women live longer than men.
10. Just the food in the dining room is for the guests and their dates.

Exercise 1b. These are suggested answers. Responses will vary.

1. While I still had eighty miles to drive, the highway was dark.
   With eighty miles still to drive, I thought the highway was too dark.
2. As I flew over San Francisco, the Golden Gate Bridge looked so awesome.
3. Coming to terms with her sexuality in light of her faith, her future looked brighter.
4. You should stretch your legs so that blood continues to circulate while you're in the wheelchair.
5. Teaching is a high-pressure field, but I still want to be a teacher.
6. Using a dry sponge, I wiped the milk from the floor.
7. The cat became terrified as my girlfriends and I rowed the boat across the lake.
8. The weather grew hotter and hotter as we watched the sun rise.
9. I want to be an engineer, even though engineering requires much mathematical ability.
10. Even though we were tired and sleepy, we still had three more hours to drive.
11. My grade was in jeopardy because I missed English class for seven days.
12. To have a good marriage, couples need to trust one another.
13. While we were standing on the side of the road, the cars almost ran over us.
14. It is difficult for an out-of-work, middle-aged man to get a date.
15. One of the greatest dates I ever had was while sitting on a bench, in a park, on a rainy night in 1996.
16. Enrique though he'd never see the day when hate crimes and school shootings were a common occurrence.
17. Looking up at the stars, the boys fell down the riverbank.
18. While I was growing up in the Deep South, the weather was always humid.
19. Hard work and commitment are qualities you need to pass your college classes.
20. It is difficult for a person with high ambition and aspirations to find someone who understands the way it is.

Exercise 2a.

1. No change
2. In order to get an "A" in their classes, many students resort to crying, screaming, and kicking.
3. No change
4. Alethea's boyfriend had tried everything he knew to win back her love – pleading, begging, crying, and buying gifts.
5. No change
6. Mosquitoes are nasty little creatures that bite, sting, stab, and suck your blood.
7. I would love to live atop a mountain, swim in the ocean, dance among the stars, and soar like an eagle.
8. Why do fools rage, evil men destroy, and the elite mock the simple?
9. No change
10. No change

Exercise 3a.

1. eliminate "By"
2. We took the old clothes we found in the attic to the church charity bazaar.
3. The teacher told the students who had all of their assignments done to stand next to their desks.
4. Mario and Julio failed their exams because of too much late night dating and too many missed classes.
5. The trainer of the tamed beasts took them to the circus owner.
6. He was irritable because he fought with his parents for two hours.
7. The best solution would be some kind of sacrifice by the citizens.
8. She sings well because she practices every day.
9. Mr. Robertson shouldn't be charged with Mrs. Robertson's murder just because he was found with the gun in his hand.
10. After a bad cut, you bleed for days.

Exercise 4a.

1. The Creeks ran with the moon in the middle of the night.
2. There were so many holes in Juan's suit pocket that he nearly lost all his money.
3. No change
4. No change
5. Maurice said they were bewildered and confused when they walked into the room.

6. It seems that teachers are always demanding and imposing.
7. Gary felt challenged when he was asked to move to London.
8. All the chaos at Riverdale High School started in 1985.
9. By now I thought both Andreas and Enrique would have left the auditorium. Or I thought both Andreas and Enrique would have left the building by now.
10. My mother always said, "You can make it if you try."

Exercise 4b.

11. Visiting the museum today are too few people.
12. There is finally a reconciliation made between Jamie and Jeremy after many disputes and arguments.
13. As the dog runs out, the cat comes in.
14. Her very wise boyfriend is my daughter's primary confidant.
15. Screeching sounds from the upstairs bedroom came during the night.
16. Visiting me today were lots of people.
17. If you get drunk and pass out, I couldn't care less.
18. Coming home from the party, Marquetta got caught.
19. For the lie Eric told, I can never forgive him.
20. These days, friends are hard to come by.

MASTERY TEST THREE

1. In many family homes, especially in southeast Georgia, all children sit down to dinner with their parents.
2. The men just stood there watching the women slide and tumble down the hill.
3. Kim thought his friend, Ralph, would make him totally insane, but Ralph ended up helping him.
4. I watched the boys and girls who were standing on a hill.
5. High school teachers generally earn more money than college professors.
6. Kimiko and Matsuo enjoy playing sports, riding bicycles, watching movies, and telling stories.
7. Mr. and Mrs. Schindler named their three daughters Faith, Hope, and Charity.
8. Helio is usually on top of the world or down in the dumps.
9. Some people want to rekindle an old love affair so badly that they will do anything from swimming the deep, blue sea to purchasing diamonds and emeralds.
10. What's more important in your life: values and principles, silver and gold, or position and power?
11. The future looked bleak for Carmen because she had ten weeks of chemotherapy ahead.
12. A career in psychiatry involves a lot of drive and determination, but I still want to be a psychiatrist.

13. You should count your blessings even when you are sad and disappointed.
14. You can find many joys while playing with your children in the park.
15. As she ran past the nurses' station in nothing but an open-backed gown, she fell into my arms.
16. We were so exhausted because we had shopped for five hours.
17. The best solution would be a compromise between the citizens of Edinburgh and the city government.
18. The best way to succeed is by obeying your parents and adhering to the Golden Rule.
19. Greg and Saba failed their classes because of too much late night carousing.
20. She interviews so well because she changes jobs every other week.
21. It was storming in the middle of the night when the lights went out and the dog ran away with the spoon.
22. When Charisse would try to lift both her arms to comb her hair, her tennis elbow got worse.
23. Mel wanted to see Linda in the early morning hours.
24. Shelby said they were dazed and confused when they heard the news of his accident.
25. They looked sad, lonely, and forlorn as they stood at the head of the casket.

CHAPTER FIVE

Exercise 1a.

1. fuzz, cops
2. bread, dough
3. ride, wheels
4. dude, guy
5. broad, babe
6. wiped out
7. starving
8. wasted, took out
9. wimp
10. super cool, large

Arthur and Pulley

Exercise 1b.

Answers will vary.

Exercise 2a.

1. baggage
2. suitcase
3. telephone
4. phone
5. execute
6. fill out

Exercise 2b.

7. I
8. F
9. I
10. F

Exercise 2c. These are suggested answers. Responses will vary.

1. survivor
2. kill herself
3. fill
4. hands
5. messy, uncoordinated, sloppy

Exercise 3a.

1. No change
2. No change
3. No change
4. Artemus swore that he would not <u>lay</u> the book down until he finished reading it.
5. It's a lovely spring day; I hope it's not going to rain, later, and spoil its splendor.
6. - 10. Answers will vary

Exercise 4a. Answers may vary.

1. Although
2. Consequently, or Subsequently,
3. In addition,
4. Furthermore,
5. Consequently, or Subsequently
6. During
7. Immediately,
8. nonetheless

Exercise 4b.

It has been awfully difficult for Justin to adjust to his newfound freedom. <u>After</u> a year of being away, he never contacts any old friends back home. <u>Since</u> he started making new friends over the Internet, he stays out half the night on weekends. <u>Now</u>, his apartment is in a mess, and his appearance is shabby. <u>Furthermore</u>, his personality is very rude and arrogant. Justin, consequently, argues and fights all the time. Meanwhile, he has begun to drink and even use drugs on a regular basis. He <u>subsequently</u> wrecked his car in a road rage encounter and was almost killed. <u>Now</u> he is in the hospital, tied to tubes and machines. <u>Moreover,</u> the doctors don't hold out much hope for his recovery. My goodness, how tragic Justin's life has become.

Exercise 5a. Answers may vary.

1. The amount of pennies collected was $800.23.
2. Boys have just as difficult a life as girls.
3. Marcella wants to date Raphael, but he keeps refusing all of her advances.
4. *The Notebook*, a short novel, was on the New York Times bestseller list for over a year.
5. If you stomp on my feet, I will cry.

Exercise 6a. Answers will vary.

1. Mariah dances <u>with enthusiasm</u> as she sings.
2. Sean often says he wants <u>a better life</u>.
3. Many frustrated people just need to <u>calm down and relax</u>.
4. Linda and Hubert were clammy and sweaty because it was <u>extremely hot</u>.
5. You need to stop <u>being outwardly emotional.</u>

Arthur and Pulley Page 283

MASTERY TEST FOUR

1. Sometimes my algebra teacher acts as if he has gone crazy.
2. I'm going to lose my boyfriend if I don't buy a car soon.
3. Yesterday, Raphael ate so much candy and got sick.
4. No change
5. Because Jonathan was so tired after his wrestling match, he lay down to rest for an hour.
6. I would rather keep my mouth shut and be thought a fool than open it and remove all doubt.
7. Their wounds from the car accident will take months to heal.
8. No change
9. No change
10. No change
11. Marshall Thomason was honored at the Tuesday night meeting.
12. Can't we all get along and be friends?
13. Maurice vowed not to date any more girls, even though he thinks they're all beautiful.
14. No change
15. It's a bad storm.
16. Jeffrey said that he was very hungry.
17. It's very hot today.
18. If you slap my face, I will cry.
19. Can't you see me among the graduates as they get their diplomas?
20. He is so phony.
21. Tristan and Kristin went on their merry way after they visited the cemetery.
22. Nick really can't appreciate that music.
23. Jessica really likes Chinese and Mexican foods.
24. Could you lie down and rest with little Susie for a while?
25. Why can't we be just friends instead of friends and lovers?

PRACTICE TEST ONE

1. B
2. A
3. A
4. D
5. C
6. C
7. D
8. B
9. D
10. B
11. A
12. B
13. A
14. D
15. C
16. C
17. D
18. B
19. C
20. D
21. D
22. B
23. A
24. B
25. D
26. B
27. B
28. C
29. D
30. B
31. D
32. D
33. C
34. B
35. C
36. A
37. B
38. C
39. B
40. D

PRACTICE TEST TWO

1. A
2. B
3. D
4. C
5. B
6. C
7. B
8. C
9. B
10. C
11. B
12. C
13. C
14. B
15. B
16. D
17. A
18. C
19. D
20. A
21. B
22. B
23. B
24. A
25. B
26. D
27. C
28. D
29. B
30. C
31. D
32. A
33. B
34. C
35. A
36. A
37. C
38. D
39. B
40. D

PRACTICE TEST THREE

1. C
2. B
3. A
4. B
5. B
6. D
7. B
8. D
9. B
10. C
11. D
12. C
13. A
14. C
15. A
16. C
17. B
18. A
19. C
20. D
21. C
22. B
23. A
24. B
25. C
26. C
27. A
28. B
29. D
30. D
31. C
32. D
33. B
34. A
35. B
36. C
37. B
38. A
39. D
40. C

PRACTICE TEST FOUR

1. C
2. D
3. B
4. D
5. C
6. B
7. C
8. D
9. A
10. D
11. D
12. B
13. D
14. A
15. B
16. C
17. A
18. A
19. D
20. A
21. A
22. D
23. D
24. B
25. C
26. A
27. C
28. D
29. B
30. A
31. A
32. D
33. B
34. C
35. C
36. C
37. B
38. D
39. C
40. B

PRACTICE TEST FIVE

1. B
2. D
3. A
4. B
5. C
6. A
7. B
8. D
9. A
10. C
11. A
12. D
13. D
14. C
15. D
16. B
17. C
18. D
19. D
20. B
21. C
22. D
23. C
24. C
25. B
26. D
27. B
28. C
29. A
30. D
31. B
32. A
33. B
34. D
35. D
36. D
37. B
38. C
39. B
40. A

PRACTICE TEST SIX

1. D
2. B
3. B
4. A
5. D
6. D
7. B
8. C
9. C
10. A
11. A
12. C
13. D
14. B
15. D
16. A
17. B
18. D
19. C
20. D
21. A
22. C
23. B
24. D
25. B
26. D
27. C
28. B
29. D
30. A
31. B
32. A
33. B
34. C
35. D
36. B
37. C
38. D
39. C
40. A

PRACTICE TEST SEVEN

1. B
2. C
3. A
4. C
5. D
6. B
7. A
8. C
9. C
10. B
11. B
12. A
13. D
14. B
15. D
16. D
17. D
18. C
19. B
20. D
21. B
22. B
23. D
24. B
25. C
26. C
27. B
28. C
29. A
30. D
31. A
32. B
33. C
34. D
35. B
36. C
37. C
38. A
39. B
40. C

PRACTICE TEST EIGHT

1. C
2. C
3. B
4. A
5. C
6. C
7. B
8. D
9. D
10. D
11. A
12. B
13. D
14. C
15. C
16. D
17. A
18. B
19. D
20. C
21. B
22. D
23. D
24. D
25. B
26. A
27. A
28. C
29. B
30. D
31. C
32. A
33. C
34. B
35. A
36. C
37. A
38. D
39. D
40. C

PRACTICE TEST NINE

1. B
2. D
3. B
4. C
5. B
6. D
7. C
8. C
9. A
10. D
11. A
12. B
13. C
14. D
15. B
16. A
17. D
18. C
19. B
20. D
21. B
22. A
23. C
24. D
25. B
26. C
27. B
28. D
29. C
30. A
31. C
32. D
33. B
34. D
35. B
36. A
37. D
38. C
39. A
40. B

PRACTICE TEST TEN

1. D
2. B
3. C
4. A
5. B
6. C
7. D
8. B
9. B
10. C
11. A
12. B
13. D
14. B
15. A
16. D
17. C
18. A
19. B
20. D
21. C
22. B
23. C
24. D
25. A
26. C
27. D
28. B
29. A
30. D
31. C
32. B
33. D
34. B
35. A
36. C
37. D
38. A
39. C
40. D

CHAPTER SIX

Answers will vary.

CHAPTER SEVEN

TYPES OF ESSAYS:

Exercise 1. but, though, although, different from, contrarily, differ, whereas, on the contrary, notwithstanding, otherwise

Exercise 2.

A. <u>For instance</u>, <u>example</u>, <u>illustration</u>
   Pattern of organization = example

B. <u>However</u>, <u>Yet</u>, <u>Contrary to</u>
   Pattern of organization = contrast

C. most miserable, bad effects; also uses card stacking
   Pattern of organization = persuasion

D. fine, black; very blue; fresh; slim; slightly built; neat; trim; grandiose; gentlemanly; cynicism; (uses lots of adjective and adverbs)
   Pattern of organization = description

Exercise 3.

1. Contrast
2. Example
3. Persuasion
4. Description
5. Persuasion
6. Description
7. Example
8. Contrast.

Exercise 4.

1. Description or example
2. Description
3. Contrast
4. Description or example
5. Persuasion
6. Example
7. Contrast
8. Contrast and description
9. Persuasion
10. Example

WRITING DESCRIPTIVE ESSAYS

Exercise 1.

"That was the worst meal I have ever eaten."

Exercise 2a.

fluffy, creamy, crisp, buttery, smooth, seasoned, golden, fried, green, tiny, crunchy

Exercise 2b.

sound- crunchy, gulped, cough, crisp
taste- like an entire box of salt
sight- buttery, green, dented, pools, golden, tiny
smell- aroma
texture (touch)- smooth, creamy, fluffy

Exercise 3

Answers will vary.

Exercise 4

Answers will vary.

WRITING AN EXAMPLE ESSAY

Exercise 1a.

father asks his child to cry and say she has stomach pains
guy says his pregnant wife/girlfriend is having a miscarriage
nervous mom says she is rushing to the pharmacy for medication
college student says he is getting medicine for sick roommate
driver says he is not well and must rush home

Exercise 1b.

for example, instance, to illustrate, example

Exercise 1c.

child-bend-grab stomach-cry; dad-pleads-"little princess"-stomach pains
nervous mom-rush-pharmacy; guy-declares-deathly ill-skipping class

Exercise 2a.

The second paragraph tells a story about a single incident and the first paragraph gives several similar examples

Exercise 2b.

patrol officer-pulls up-blue lights flashing-sirens screaming-loudly
driver-desperately-think-perfect excuse; sister-driving-Mississippi-Georgia
patrol officer-turned around-grassy median; we- panicked; she-pled-case-traffic court-Massachusetts

Exercise 2c.

Answers will vary.

Exercise 3

Answers will vary.

Exercise 4

Answers will vary.

WRITING PERSUASIVE ESSAYS

Exercise 1

sports celebrities

Exercise 2a.

against college athletes accepting professional sports' contracts and not graduating from college rationale
examples about actual professional athletes and their injuries

Exercise 2b.

Examples and facts
Cedric Henderson-right sprained ankle - out indefinitely; Rice- torn tendon- surgery- out for the year; Shea Ralph-knee surgery- has torn ACL five times

Exercise 3

Answers will vary.

Exercise 4

Answers will vary.

WRITING CONTRAST ESSAYS

Exercise 1a.

Other points about amusement parks: food, shows, cost of tickets, cartoon characters featured

Exercise 1b.

Answers will vary.

Exercise 2a.

difference, on the other hand, contrasted

Exercise 2b.

Disney World:
(location) Orlando, Florida (size) thousands attend, enormous, five parks, several miles, (rides) special rides- magic carpet, safari, tower of terror

Six Flags:
(location) Atlanta, Georgia (size) hundreds attend, smaller, one park, several acres (rides) mostly roller coasters

Exercise 3

Answers will vary.

Exercise 4

Answers will vary.

REFERENCES FOR CHAPTERS

CHAPTER ONE

Arthur, Linda L., Donna Hooley, and Michael Mills. *Making the Most of Your Southern Experience.* Needham Heights: Simon and Schuster, 1996.

CHAPTER FIVE

Salem, Dorothy C. *The Journey: A History of the African American Experience.* Dubuque: Kendall/Hunt Publishing, 1997.

CHAPTER SIX

Arthur, Linda L. and Mark Dallas. *Reading for College.* Dubuque: Kendall Hunt Publishing, 1999.

Baron, Robert A. *Essentials of Psychology.* 2nd edition. Boston: Allyn and Bacon, 1999.

Smith, Brenda. *Breaking Through: College Reading.* 6th edition. New York: Addison, Wesley, Longman Publishers, 2002.

CHAPTER SEVEN

Fowles, James. *French Lieutenant's Woman.* New York: Penguin, 1970.

Jackson, Donald Dale. "The Art of Wishful Shrinking." In *Reading Passages* by Carolyn H. Fitzpatrick and Marybeth B. Ruscica (eds.) Boston: Houghton Mifflin, 1997.

Shepherd, Mary L. "Granville T. Woods: The Successful Dropout." In *Blacks in Ohio: Seven Portraits* by John B. McClusky's (ed.) Cleveland: The New Day Press, 1976.

Vickery, Donald, M.D. and James Fries, M.D. *Taking Care of Yourself.* 6th ed. New York: Addison-Wesley, 1996.

Zigler, Edward F. "Language Development." In *Reading Passages* by Carolyn H. Fitzpatrick and Marybeth B. Ruscica (eds.) Boston: Houghton Mifflin, 1997.

REFERENCES FOR PRACTICE EXIT EXAMS
[Please note that passages have been adapted to facilitate testing exercises]

PRACTICE EXIT EXAM ONE

Albanese, Jay. *Criminal Justice.* 2nd ed. Boston: Allyn and Bacon, 2002.
Hoffman, Matthew. *Book of Home Remedies for Dogs and Cats.* New York: Bantam Books, 1996.
Martin, James, et al. *America and Its Peoples.* New York: Addison Wesley Longman, Inc., 1997.
Seton, Anya. *Katherine.* New York: Houghton Mifflin, 1954.

PRACTICE EXIT EXAM TWO

Fraser, Antonia. *The Lives of the Kings and Queens of England.* New York: Alfred A. Knopf, 1975.
Grizzard, Lewis. *Shoot Low Boys – They're Ridin' Shetland Ponies.* New York: Ballantine Books, 1985.
Gurian, Michael. *The Wonder of Boys.* New York: Penguin Putnam, Inc., 1996.
Wilkins, David, Bernard Schultz, and Katheryn M. Linduff. *Art Past, Art Present.* 2nd ed. Englewood Cliffs: Prentice Hall, 1994.

PRACTICE EXIT EXAM THREE

King, Betty. *The Captive James.* London: Herbert Jenkins, 1967.
Pipher, Mary. *Reviving Ophelia: Saving the Selves of Adolescent Girls.* New York: Ballantine Books, 1994.
Sams, Jamie and David Carson. *Medicine Cards.* Santa Fe: Bear and Company, 1988.
Wallace, Ian. *Reflections on Scotland.* Norwich: Jarrold Publications, 1988.

PRACTICE EXIT EXAM FOUR

Anaya. *Bless Me, Ultima.* Berkeley: TQS Publications, 1972.
Dorenkamp, Angela, John F. McClymer, Mary M. Maynikan, and Arlene C. Vadum. *Images of Women in American Popular Culture.* New York: Harcourt, Brace, and Jovanivich, 1985.
Freeman, Arthur and Rose DeWolf. *10 Dumbest Mistakes Smart People Make.* New York: Harper Perennial, 1992.
Let's Go. London: Macmillan, 2000.

PRACTICE EXIT EXAM FIVE

Bender, David and Bruno Leone. *Male/Female Roles: Opposing Viewpoints.* San Diego: Greenhaven Press, Inc., 1989.
Erickson, Joan (Ed.). *Australia Travel Guide.* Menlo Park: Lane Publishing Co., 1987.
O'brien, Alexandra A. "Death in Ancient Egypt." *Research Archives.* Chicago: The Oriental Institute, 1999 or internet address: http://www.-oi.uchicago.edu/OI/DEPT/RA/ABZU/DEATH.html.
Olson-Fallon, Judith. *Growing Up, Growing Old.* New York: Harper Collins College Publishers, 1992.

PRACTICE EXIT EXAM SIX

Bowen, John R. *Religions in Practice: An Approach to the Anthropology of Religion.* Boston: Allyn and Bacon, 1998.
Fawcett, Susan and Alvin Sandberg. *Evergreen with Reading.* 4th ed. Boston: Houghton Mifflin, 1992.
Keboe, Thomas, et al. *Exploring Western Civilization to 1648.* Dubuque: Kendall/Hunt Publishing Company, 1997.
Null, Gary. *The Women's Encyclopedia of Natural Healing.* New York: Seven Stories Press, 1996.

PRACTICE EXIT EXAM SEVEN

Lappe, Frances Moore and Joseph Collins. *World Hunger: Twelve Myths.* New York: Grove Weidenfeld, 1986.
Nydell, Margaret K. *Understanding Arabs: A Guide for Westerners.* Yarmouth, Maine: Intercultural Press, Inc., 1987.
Salem, Dorothy C. *The Journey.* Dubuque: Kendall Hunt Publishing Company, 1997.
White, E. B. *Charlotte's Web.* New York: Harper and Row, Publishers, 1957.

PRACTICE EXIT EXAM EIGHT

Couto, Richard and Nancy B. Stutts and Associates. *Mending Broken Promises: Justice for Children at Risk.* Dubuque: Kendall/Hunt Publishing Company, 2000.
Haroldsen, Mark O. *How to Wake Up the Financial Genius Inside You.* Toronto: Bantam Books, 1984.
Nierenberg, Gerald and Henry Calero. *How to Read a Person Like a Book.* New York: Pocket Books, 1971.
Troyat, Henri. *Catherine the Great.* Trans. by Joan Pinkham. New York: E P Dutton, 1980.

PRACTICE EXIT EXAM NINE

Harris, Thomas A. *I'm OK – You're OK.* New York: Avon Books, 1973.
Katzenstein, Gary. *Funny Business.* New York: Prentice-Hall, 1989.
Office of the Prime Minister. *Thailand in the 90s.* Royal Thai Government, 1991.
Valentine, Michael R. *Difficult Discipline Problems: A Family-Systems Approach.* Dubuque: Kendall/Hunt Publishing Company, 1988.

PRACTICE EXIT EXAM TEN

Chillingham Castle. "Ghosts, Hauntings and Apparitions, Northumberland, North East England." Internet Address: http://www.chillingham-castle.com.
Kestner, Jane, et. al. *General Psychology.* Dubuque: Kendall/Hunt Publishing Company, 2001.
Mead, Marion. *Stealing Heaven: The Love Story of Heloise and Abelard.* New York: Soho Press, Inc., 1979.